Register Your Book
at ibmpressbooks.com/ibmregister

Upon registration, we will send you electronic sample chapters from two of our popular IBM Press books. In addition, you will be automatically entered into a monthly drawing for a free IBM Press book.

Registration also entitles you to:

- Notices and reminders about author appearances, conferences, and online chats with special guests

- Access to supplemental material that may be available

- Advance notice of forthcoming editions

- Related book recommendations

- Information about special contests and promotions throughout the year

- Chapter excerpts and supplements of forthcoming books

Contact us

If you are interested in writing a book or reviewing manuscripts prior to publication, please write to us at:

Editorial Director, IBM Press
c/o Pearson Education
800 East 96th Street
Indianapolis, IN 46240

e-mail: IBMPress@pearsoned.com

Visit us on the Web: ibmpressbooks.com

Visual Modeling with IBM® Rational® Software Architect and UML™

The IBM Press developerWorks Series represents a unique undertaking in which print books and the Web are mutually supportive. The publications in this series are complemented by their association with resources available at the developerWorks Web site on ibm.com. These resources include articles, tutorials, forums, software, and much more.

Through the use of icons, readers will be able to immediately identify a resource on developerWorks which relates to that point of the text. A summary of links appears at the end of each chapter. Additionally, you will be able to access an electronic guide of the developerWorks links and resources through ibm.com/developerworks/dwbooks that reference developerWorks Series publications, deepening the reader's experiences.

A developerWorks book offers readers the ability to quickly extend their information base beyond the book by using the deep resources of developerWorks and at the same time enables developerWorks readers to deepen their technical knowledge and skills.

For a full listing of developerWorks Series publications, please visit: **ibmpressbooks.com/dwseries**.

WebSphere® Books

IBM® WebSphere®
Barcia, Hines, Alcott, and Botzum

IBM® WebSphere® Application Server for Distributed Platforms and z/OS®
Black, Everett, Draeger, Miller, Iyer, McGuinnes, Patel, Herescu, Gissel, Betancourt, Casile, Tang, and Beaubien

Enterprise Java™ Programming with IBM® WebSphere®, Second Edition
Brown, Craig, Hester, Pitt, Stinehour, Weitzel, Amsden, Jakab, and Berg

IBM® WebSphere® and Lotus
Lamb, Laskey, and Indurkhya

IBM® WebSphere® System Administration
Williamson, Chan, Cundiff, Lauzon, and Mitchell

Enterprise Messaging Using JMS and IBM® WebSphere®
Yusuf

On Demand Computing Books

Business Intelligence for the Enterprise
Biere

On Demand Computing
Fellenstein

Grid Computing
Joseph and Fellenstein

Autonomic Computing
Murch

Rational® Software Books

Software Configuration Management Strategies and IBM Rational ClearCase®, Second Edition
Bellagio and Milligan

More Books from IBM Press

Irresistible! Markets, Models, and Meta-Value in Consumer Electronics
Bailey and Wenzek

Service-Oriented Architecture Compass
Bieberstein, Bose, Fiammante, Jones, and Shah

Developing Quality Technical Information, Second Edition
Hargis, Carey, Hernandez, Hughes, Longo, Rouiller, and Wilde

Performance Tuning for Linux® Servers
Johnson, Huizenga, and Pulavarty

RFID Sourcebook
Lahiri

Building Applications with the Linux Standard Base
Linux Standard Base Team

An Introduction to IMS™
Meltz, Long, Harrington, Hain, and Nicholls

Search Engine Marketing, Inc.
Moran and Hunt

Inescapable Data
Stakutis and Webster

DB2® Books

DB2® Universal Database V8 for Linux, UNIX, and Windows Database Administration Certification Guide, Fifth Edition
Baklarz and Wong

Understanding DB2®
Chong, Liu, Qi, and Snow

Integrated Solutions with DB2®
Cutlip and Medicke

High Availability Guide for DB2®
Eaton and Cialini

DB2® Universal Database V8 Handbook for Windows, UNIX, and Linux
Gunning

DB2® SQL PL, Second Edition
Janmohamed, Liu, Bradstock, Chong, Gao, McArthur, and Yip

DB2® Universal Database for OS/390 V7.1 Application Certification Guide
Lawson

DB2® for z/OS® Version 8 DBA Certification Guide
Lawson

DB2® Universal Database V8 Application Development Certification Guide, Second Edition
Martineau, Sanyal, Gashyna, and Kyprianou

DB2® Universal Database V8.1 Certification Exam 700 Study Guide
Sanders

DB2® Universal Database V8.1 Certification Exam 703 Study Guide
Sanders

DB2® Universal Database V8.1 Certification Exams 701 and 706 Study Guide
Sanders

DB2® Universal Database for OS/390
Sloan and Hernandez

The Official Introduction to DB2® for z/OS®, Second Edition
Sloan

Advanced DBA Certification Guide and Reference for DB2® Universal Database v8 for Linux, UNIX, and Windows
Snow and Phan

DB2® Express
Yip, Cheung, Gartner, Liu, and O'Connell

Apache Derby — Off to the Races
Zikopoulos, Baklarz, and Scott

DB2® Version 8
Zikopoulos, Baklarz, deRoos, and Melnyk

Visual Modeling with IBM® Rational® Software Architect and UML™

developerWorks® Series

Terry Quatrani

Jim Palistrant

IBM Press
Pearson plc
Upper Saddle River, NJ • Boston • Indianapolis • San Francisco
New York • Toronto • Montreal • London • Munich • Paris • Madrid
Capetown • Sydney • Tokyo • Singapore • Mexico City
ibmpressbooks.com

Published by Pearson plc
Publishing as IBM Press

IBM Press offers excellent discounts on this book when ordered in quantity for bulk purchases or special sales, which may include electronic versions and/or custom covers and content particular to your business, training goals, marketing focus, and branding interests. For more information, please contact:

U.S. Corporate and Government Sales
1-800-382-3419
corpsales@pearsontechgroup.com

For sales outside the United States, please contact:

International Sales
international@pearsoned.com

 This Book Is Safari Enabled

The Safari® Enabled icon on the cover of your favorite technology book means the book is available through Safari Bookshelf. When you buy this book, you get free access to the online edition for 45 days.

Safari Bookshelf is an electronic reference library that lets you easily search thousands of technical books, find code samples, download chapters, and access technical information whenever and wherever you need it.

To gain 45-day Safari Enabled access to this book:

• Go to http://www.awprofessional.com/safarienabled

• Complete the brief registration form

• Enter the coupon code NMAR-B3SB-UGYW-N6BA-56ZI

If you have difficulty registering on Safari Bookshelf or accessing the online edition, please e-mail customer-service@safaribooksonline.com.

Library of Congress Cataloging-in-Publication Data
Quatrani, Terry.
  Visual modeling with IBM® Rational® software architect and UML™ / Terry Quatrani, Jim Palistrant.
      p. cm.
   Includes index.
   ISBN 0-321-23808-7 (pbk. : alk. paper)
   1. Visual programming (Computer science) 2. Software architecture. 3. System design. 4. UML (Computer science) I. Palistrant, Jim. II. Title.
   QA76.65.Q395 2006
   005.1'18—dc22
                                                        2006013032

ISBN 0-321-23808-7
Text printed in the United States on recycled paper at RR Donnelly in Crawfordsville, Indiana.
First printing, May 2006

The continuation of this copyright page, including trademark and other information, is on page 194.

Contents

Foreword

When Jim Rumbaugh, Ivar Jacobson, and I set out to define the original version of the Unified Modeling Language (UML), we observed then—as we still do now—that the role of the UML was to "visualize, specify, construct, and document the artifacts of a software-intensive system." Notice our emphasis on visualization: we visualize in order to reason about complex structures and behavior. By choosing the right visualization, we are able to rise above the details of specific implementation languages and other technologies so that we can specify, construct, and document the patterns and the multitude of other design decisions that shape a system's architecture.

Now, the term "architecture" is an emotionally laden term. To some, it represents a heavyweight artifact of a high-ceremony process; to others, it's just the same as design. For me, however, software architecture represents the significant design decisions that form a software-intensive system; all software architecture is design, but not all design is software architecture. Furthermore, my experience has been that every such system has an architecture, although some are intentional while others are accidental. Nonetheless, every successful organization tends to grow its system's architecture incrementally and iteratively.

I've had the pleasure of working with Terry for many years, and she deeply understands the importance and the practice of visualizing with the UML. In this book, she focuses on visualizing various aspects of a system's architecture as it grows through the life cycle, from use cases at inception through analysis, design, implementation, and even test cases during elaboration and implementation.

Terry's style is always direct, approachable, and pragmatic. Abstraction is hard, and visualizing abstractions is yet another hard problem, but here she'll guide you in doing both using Rational Software Architect.

Grady Booch
IBM Fellow

Preface

When I set out to write the first version of this book, I thought, "This should be pretty easy . . . I do this for a living." Boy, was I wrong! Putting into words what I do on a daily basis was one of the hardest things I had ever done (all right, childbirth was more painful, but not by much). But I persevered, spent many, many nights and weekends in front of my computer, and gave birth to *Visual Modeling with Rational Rose and UML*. I must admit that the first time I saw my book on the bookshelf at a local bookstore, I was thrilled. I also found out that you need to have very thick skin to read book reviews. My book is unique since people seem to love it (5 stars) or they are less than impressed with it (1 star). For some reason, I rarely get a rating in between.

I have also figured out that writing a book that is tied to a tool is like rearing a child—it needs constant care. So, once again, I spent hours in front of my computer updating my book to adhere to the features found in Rational Rose 2002.

Then development went and changed things again and came out with a brand new tool . . . the joys of progress. So, a new tool meant another new book. This time I got smarter and added a coauthor. Just like my first time around, Jim thought this would be easy. Boy was he surprised! And since I have compared writing to childbirth, I can definitely tell you that Jim is very glad he can never experience that pain.

GOAL

AS FAR AS the two camps of reviewers, nothing will change there. If you liked my other books, you will like this one, since the aim of the book has not changed: to be a simple introduction to the world of visual modeling. In fact, you may even like it more since we actually take it into code development this time. If you were less than impressed with the first two books, you will probably not like this one either. I say this since the goal of the book has not changed. It is not a complete guide to the UML (these books have been written by Grady and Jim, and I am not even going to attempt to compete with the definitive experts). It is not a complete guide to the Rational Unified Process (these books have been written, quite nicely, by other people). It is not even a complete book on code development. As I stated, this book is meant to take a simple, first look at how a process, a language, and a tool may be used to create a blueprint of your system.

APPROACH

THIS BOOK TAKES a practical approach to teaching visual modeling techniques and the UML. It uses a case study to show the analysis, design, and a bit of implementation of an application. The application is a course registration system for a university. This problem domain was chosen because it is understood easily and is not specific to any field of computer science. You can concentrate on the specifics of modeling the domain rather than investing time in understanding an unfamiliar problem domain.

The problem is treated seriously enough to give you practical exercise with visual modeling techniques and the feeling for solving a real problem, without being so realistic that you are bogged down in details. Thus many interesting and perhaps necessary requirements, considerations, and constraints were put aside to produce a simplified, yet useful case study fitting the scope of this book.

MORE AT DEVELOPERWORKS

FOR ADDITIONAL DETAILS on visual modeling and the UML or on applying the techniques to your application, we have added pointers to articles that can be found in the Rational section of developerWorks (www.ibm.com/developerWorks/rational).

CHAPTER SUMMARIES

THIS SECTION PROVIDES brief overviews of each of the chapters.

Chapter 1: Introduction to Visual Modeling

This chapter introduces the techniques, language, and process that are used throughout the book. It discusses the benefits of visual modeling, the history of the UML, and the software development process used.

Chapter 2: Beginning a Project

Chapter 2 simply contains information that is related to the Course Registration System case study that is used throughout the book.

Chapter 3: The Use Case Model

This chapter discusses the techniques used to examine system behavior from a use case approach. It shows how to visually capture and document the functional requirements of your system.

Chapter 4: The Analysis Model

In this chapter we discuss the techniques used to create the analysis model, which is the first step down the path of system implementation. This is the first model that starts to enable you to see "how" the system will be implemented.

Chapter 5: The Design Model

This chapter discusses the techniques used to create the design model. The design model is the realization of the analysis model and serves as an abstration of the implementation model and its source code.

Chapter 6: Implementation Model

Here we discuss the techniques used to create the implementation model. The implementation model represents the physical composition of the implementation in terms of implementation subsystems and implementation elements (directories and files, including source code, data, and executable files). As Jim never fails to remind me, "Something has to run."

Appendix A: UML Metamodel

This appendix discusses the changes made to the UML metamodel for UML 2.0

Appendix B: Notation Summary

Appendix B illustrates UML 2.0 notation.

ACKNOWLEDGMENTS

WE WOULD LIKE to thank a number of individuals for their contributions to the content, style, presentation, and writing of this book.

Special thanks to the following people: Grady Booch, Jim Conallen, Maria Ericsson, Kurt Bittner, Ivar Jacobson, Philippe Kruchten, Peter Luckey, Walker Royce, Jim Rumbaugh, Tom Schultz, Anthony Kesterson, George DeCandio, Rick Weaver, Eric Naiburg. We would also like to thank the kind people at IBM Press—Bill Zobrist,

Mary Kate Murray, and Chris Zahn—for without their help this book would never have gone to print. Finally, Jim would like to thank the folks at his local Caribou Coffee shop for keeping him properly caffeinated.

About the Authors

Terry Quatrani is the UML Evangelist at IBM Corporation. Terry travels the world preaching the visual modeling gospel according to Grady Booch, Jim Rumbaugh, and Ivar Jacobson. She is the coauthor of the book *Succeeding with the Booch and OMT Methods* (1996) and the author of the bestselling books *Visual Modeling with Rational Rose and UML* (1998), *Visual Modeling with Rational Rose 2000 and UML* (2000), and *Visual Modeling with Rational Rose 2002 and UML* (2003), all from Addison-Wesley.

Prior to working for IBM, Terry was employed by Rational Software Corporation, where she was the UML Evangelist, and General Electric Company, where she was a founding member of the GE Advanced Concepts Center as well as a programmer and analyst. She started her professional career as an eighth grade math teacher in Pennsauken, New Jersey. Terry has a bachelor of science degree in mathematics from St. Joseph's University in Philadelphia, Pennsylvania.

Jim Palistrant has been working on development and test tools for most of his 25-year IBM career, with experiences ranging from assembler language system programming to object-oriented languages. He started working on IBM's Java and Web development tools in 1995, helping to bring various flavors of IBM's development tools to market. He has most recently been working on SOA-related tools. He has a bachelor's degree in information systems and a master's degree in computer science from the University of North Carolina.

Introduction to Visual Modeling

1

VISUAL MODELING IS a way of thinking about problems using models organized around real-world ideas. Models are useful for understanding problems, communicating with everyone involved with the project (customers, domain experts, analysts, designers, etc.), modeling enterprises, preparing documentation, and designing programs and databases. Modeling promotes better understanding of requirements, cleaner designs, and more maintainable systems.

Models are abstractions that portray the essentials of a complex problem or structure by filtering out nonessential details, thus making the problem easier to understand. Abstraction is a fundamental human capability that permits us to deal with complexity. Engineers, artists, and craftsmen have built models for thousands of years to try out designs before executing them. Development of software systems should be no exception. To build complex systems, the developer must abstract different views of the system, build models using precise notations, verify that the models satisfy the requirements of the system, and gradually add detail to transform the models into an implementation.

We build models of complex systems because we cannot comprehend such systems in their entirety. There are limits to the human capacity to understand complexity. This concept may be seen in the world of architecture. If you want to build a shed in your backyard, you can just start building; if you want to build a new house, you probably need a blueprint; if you are building a skyscraper, you definitely need a blueprint. The same is true in the world of software. Staring at lines of source code or even analyzing forms in Visual Basic does little to provide the programmer with a global view of a development project. Constructing a model allows the designer to focus on the big picture of how a project's components interact, without having to get bogged down in the specific details of each component.

Increasing complexity, resulting from a highly competitive and ever-changing business environment, offers unique challenges to system developers. Models help us organize, visualize, understand, and create complex things. They are used to help us meet the challenges of developing software today and in the future.

THE TRIANGLE FOR SUCCESS

I HAVE OFTEN used the triangle for success as shown in Figure 1-1 to explain the components needed for a successful project. You need all three facets—a notation, a process, and a tool. You can learn a notation, but if you don't know how to use it (process), you will probably fail. You may have a great process, but if you can't communicate the process (notation), you will probably fail. And lastly, if you cannot document the artifacts of your work (tool), you will probably fail.

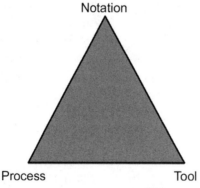

Figure 1-1   Triangle for Success

THE ROLE OF NOTATION

NOTATION PLAYS AN important part in any model—it is the glue that holds the process together. "Notation has three roles:

- It serves as the language for communicating decisions that are not obvious or cannot be inferred from the code itself.

- It provides semantics that are rich enough to capture all important strategic and tactical decisions.

- It offers a form concrete enough for humans to reason and for tools to manipulate."[1]

The Unified Modeling Language (UML) provides a very robust notation, which grows from analysis into design. Certain elements of the notation (for example, classes, associations, aggregations, inheritance) are introduced during analysis. Other elements of the notation (for example, containment implementation indicators and properties) are introduced during design.

HISTORY OF THE UML

R.1.1

DURING THE 1990S many different methodologies, along with their own set of notations, were introduced to the market. Three of the most popular methods were OMT (Rumbaugh), Booch, and OOSE (Jacobson). Each method had its own value and emphasis. OMT was strong in analysis and weaker in the design area. Booch 1991 was strong in design and weaker in analysis. Jacobson was strong in behavior analysis and weaker in the other areas.

---

1. Booch, Grady. *Object Solutions.* Reading, MA: Addison-Wesley, 1996.

As time moved on, Booch wrote his second book, which adopted a lot of the good analysis techniques advocated by Rumbaugh and Jacobson, among others. Rumbaugh published a series of articles that have become known as OMT-2 that adopted a lot of the good design techniques of Booch. The methods were beginning to converge but they still had their own unique notations. The use of different notations brought confusion to the market since one symbol meant different things to different people. For example, a filled circle was a multiplicity indicator in OMT and an aggregation symbol in Booch. You will hear the term "method wars" being used to describe this period of time—is a class a cloud or a rectangle? Which one is better?

The end of the method wars as far as notation is concerned came with the adoption of the Unified Modeling Language (UML). "UML is a language used to specify, visualize, and document the artifacts of an object-oriented system under development. It represents the unification of the Booch, OMT, and Objectory notations, as well as the best ideas from a number of other methodologists as shown in Figure 1-2. By unifying the notations used by these object-oriented methods, the Unified Modeling Language provides the basis for a *de facto* standard in the domain of object-oriented analysis and design founded on a wide base of user experience."[2]

The UML is an attempt to standardize the artifacts of analysis and design: semantic models, syntactic notation, and diagrams. The first public draft (version 0.8) was introduced in October 1995. Feedback from the public and Ivar Jacobson's input were included in the next two versions (0.9

---

2. *The Unified Method*, Draft Edition (0.8). Rational Software Corporation, October, 1995.

in July 1996 and 0.91 in October 1996). Version 1.0 was presented to the Object Management Group (OMG) for standardization in July 1997. Additional enhancements were incorporated into the 1.1 version of UML, which was presented to the OMG in September 1997. In November 1997, the UML was adopted as the standard modeling language by the OMG. At the writing of this book, UML is being updated to UML 2.0. This work is being done in four parts: UML 2.0 Superstructure, UML 2.0 Infrastructure, UML 2.0 Object Constraint Language (OCL) and UML 2.0 Diagram Interchange. Adoption of the UML 2.0 Superstructure (document that describes the UML notation) is complete and is just going through a final editing phase (no techical changes can be done to the specification). Work on the other three documents is nearly complete. You can find more information on the UML by visiting the OMG website at www.omg.org.

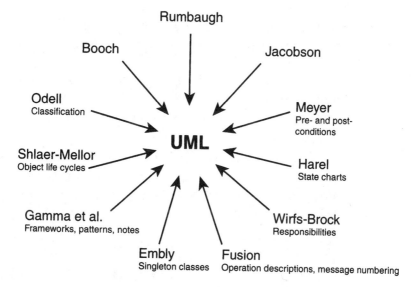

Figure 1-2   UML Inputs

THE ROLE OF PROCESS

A SUCCESSFUL DEVELOPMENT project satisfies or exceeds the customer's expectations, is developed in a timely and economical fashion, and is resilient to change and adaptation. The development life cycle must promote creativity and innovation. At the same time, the development process must be controlled and measured to ensure that the project is indeed completed. "Creativity is essential to the crafting of all well-structured object-oriented architectures, but developers allowed completely unrestrained creativity tend to never reach closure. Similarly, discipline is required when organizing the efforts of a team of developers, but too much discipline gives birth to an ugly bureaucracy that kills all attempts at innovation."[3] A well-managed iterative and incremental life cycle provides the necessary control without affecting creativity.

WHAT IS ITERATIVE AND INCREMENTAL DEVELOPMENT?

IN AN ITERATIVE and incremental life cycle (Figure 1-3), development proceeds as a series of iterations that evolve into the final system. Each iteration consists of one or more of the following process components: business modeling, requirements, analysis, design, implementation, test, and deployment. The developers do not assume that all requirements are known at the beginning of the life cycle; indeed, change is anticipated throughout all phases.

This type of life cycle is a risk-mitigating process. Technical risks are assessed and prioritized early in the life cycle and are revised during the development of each iteration.

---

3. Booch, Grady. *Object Solutions*. Reading, MA: Addison-Wesley, 1996.

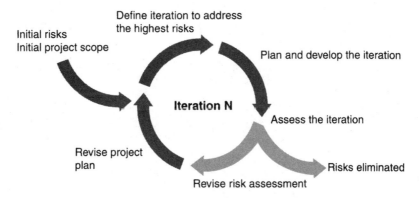

Figure 1-3   Iterative and Incremental Development

Risks are attached to each iteration so that successful completion of the iteration alleviates the risks attached to it. The releases are scheduled to ensure that the highest risks are tackled first. Building the system in this fashion exposes and mitigates the risks of the system early in the life cycle. The result of this life cycle approach is less risk coupled with minimal investment.[4]

THE RATIONAL UNIFIED PROCESS

R.1.2

CONTROL FOR AN iterative and incremental life cycle is supported by employing the Rational Unified Process—an extensive set of guidelines that address the technical and organizational aspects of software development, focusing on requirements analysis and design.

---

4. More information on the application of an iterative and incremental approach to software development may be found in the article "A Rational Development Process" by Philippe Kruchten, *CrossTalk*, 9(7), July 1996, pp. 11–16. This paper is also available on the Rational website: http://www.rational.com.

The Rational Unified Process is structured along two dimensions:

- Time—division of the life cycle into phases and iterations

- Process components—production of a specific set of artifacts with well-defined activities

Both dimensions must be taken into account for a project to succeed.

Structuring a project along the time dimension involves the adoption of the following time-based phases:

- Inception—specifying the project vision

- Elaboration—planning the necessary activities and required resources; specifying the features and designing the architecture

- Construction—building the product as a series of incremental iterations

- Transition—supplying the product to the user community (manufacturing, delivering, and training)

Structuring the project along the process component dimension includes the following activities:

- Business modeling—the identification of desired system capabilities and user needs

- Requirements—a narration of the system vision along with a set of functional and nonfunctional requirements

- Analysis and design—a description of how the system will be realized in the Implementation phase

- Implementation—the production of the code that will result in an executable system

- Test—the verification of the entire system
- Deployment—the delivery of the system and user training to the customer

Figure 1-4 shows how the process components are applied to each time-based phase.

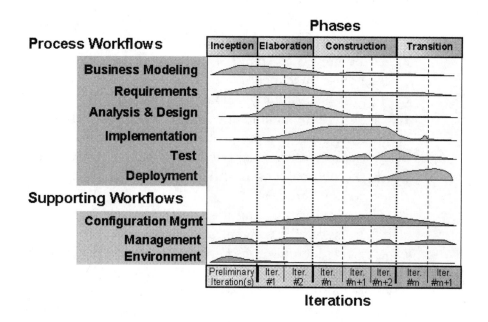

Figure 1-4   The Development Process

Each activity of the process component dimension typically is applied to each phase of the time-based dimension. However, the degree to which a particular process component is applied is dependent upon the phase of development. For example, you may decide to do a proof of concept prototype during the Inception phase, and thus, you will be doing more than just capturing requirements (you will be doing the analysis, design, implementation, and test needed to complete the prototype). The majority of the analysis process component occurs during the Elaboration phase. However, it is also advisable to complete the first few iterations of the system during this phase. These first few iterations typically are used to validate the analysis decisions made for the architecture of the system. Hence, you are doing more than just analyzing the problem. During the Construction phase of development, the system is completed as a series of iterations. As with any type of development structure, things always crop up as the system is built; thus, you are still doing some analysis.

The diagram is meant to be a guideline for the life cycle of your project. The main point is if you are still trying to figure out what you are supposed to be building as you are writing the code, you are probably in trouble. You should also note that testing is applied throughout the iteration process—you do not wait until all the code is done to see if it all works together!

This book uses a simplified version of the Rational Unified Process, which concentrates on the use of the UML to capture and document the decisions made during the Inception and Elaboration phases of development. The last few chapters lightly cover construction of the system. Although testing is a very integral part of system development, it is beyond the scope of this book.

RATIONAL SOFTWARE ARCHITECT

R.1.3
R.1.4

ANY SOFTWARE DEVELOPMENT method is best supported by a tool. When I first started OO modeling, my tool was paper and a pencil, which left a lot to be desired. There are many tools on the market today—everything from simple drawing tools to sophisticated object modeling tools. This book makes use of the tool Rational Software Architect. At every step, there is a description of how to use Rational Software Architect to complete the step. If you are only interested in modeling (chapters 3 and 4), Rational Software Modeler may be used. You can find more information about these tools, including evaluation editions, at www.ibm.com.

SUMMARY

VISUAL MODELING IS a way of thinking about problems using models organized around real-world ideas. Models are useful for understanding problems, communication, modeling enterprises, preparing documentation, and designing programs and databases. Modeling promotes better understanding of requirements, cleaner designs, and more maintainable systems. Notation plays an important part in any model—it is the glue that holds the process together. The Unified Modeling Language (UML) provides a very robust notation, which grows from analysis into design.

A successful development project satisfies or exceeds the customer's expectations, is developed in a timely and economical fashion, and is resilient to change and adaptation. The development life cycle must promote creativity and innovation. A well-managed iterative and incremental life cycle provides the necessary control without affecting creativity. In an iterative and incremental development life cycle, development proceeds as a series of iterations that evolve into the final system. Each iteration consists of one or more of the following process components: business modeling, requirements, analysis, design, implementation, test, and deployment.

Control for an iterative and incremental life cycle is provided in the Rational Unified Process—an extensive set of guidelines that address the technical and organizational aspects of software development, focusing on requirements analysis and design. This book uses a simplified version of the Rational Unified Process.

Rational Software Architect is a design and construction tool for creating applications for the Java platform or in C++ that leverages model-driven development with the UML (Unified Modeling Language) and unifies all aspects of software application architecture.

DEVELOPERWORKS LINKS

R.1.1 UML Resource page (OMG official Unified Modeling Language resources): http://www.uml.org/

R.1.2 developerWorks Rational area for material about Rational methodology and tools: http://www-128.ibm.com/developerworks/rational

R.1.3 Rational Software Architect area on developerWorks, including downloads, support, examples, how-to articles, documentation: http://www-128.ibm.com/developerworks/rational/products/rsa/

R.1.4 Rational Software Architect discussion forum: http://www-128.ibm.com/developerworks/forums/dw_forum.jsp?forum=430&cat=24

2

Beginning a Project

DEFINING THE RIGHT PROJECT

THE MOST IMPORTANT question to ask when developing a system is not a methodological question. It is not a technical question. It is a seemingly simple, yet remarkably difficult question: "Is this the right system to make?" Unfortunately, this question is often never asked nor answered. Although misguided methodology or technically tough problems can cause projects to fail, sufficient resources and heroic effort by talented people often can save them. But nothing can save a system that is not needed or that automates the wrong thing.

Before starting a project, there must be an idea for it. The process of coming up with an idea for a system along with a general idea of its requirements and form occurs during the Inception phase. It finishes the statement: "The system we want does . . ." During this phase of development, a vision for the idea is established, and many assumptions are either validated or rejected. Activities that occur involve the solicitation of ideas, the preliminary identification of risks, the identification of external interfaces, the identification of the major functionality that must be provided by the system, and possibly some "proof of concept" prototypes. Ideas come from many sources: customers, domain experts, other developers, industry experts, feasibility studies, and review of existing systems. It is important to note that any prototyping done during this phase should be considered throw-away code since the code generated is merely to support a list of assumptions and has not been fully analyzed or designed.

The process used during this phase of development can be done formally or informally, but it always involves considering the business needs, the available resources, the possible technology, and the user-community desires along with several ideas for new systems. Brainstorming, research, trade studies, cost-benefit analysis, use case analysis, and prototyping can then be performed to produce the target system's concept along with defined purposes, priorities, and context. Usually, a first-pass cut at resource and schedule planning is also done during this phase. For some projects, the product vision can be sketched on the back of a napkin. For others, the product vision may be a formal phase that is iteratively performed until enough level of detail of the target system has been specified.

An adequate Inception phase establishes the high-level requirements for a desirable and feasible system, both technologically and sociologically. An inadequate Inception phase leads to systems so unwanted, expensive, impossible, and ill-defined that they are typically never finished or used.

EASTERN STATE UNIVERSITY (ESU) BACKGROUND

THE ESU COURSE registration problem will be used as an example throughout this book.

The process of assigning professors to courses and the registration of students is a frustrating and time-consuming experience.

After the professors of ESU have decided which courses they are going to teach for the semester, the Registrar's office enters the information into the computer system. A batch report is printed for the professors indicating which courses they will teach. A course catalog is printed and distributed to the students.

The students currently fill out (multipart, multicolor) registration forms that indicate their choice in courses, and return the completed forms to the Registrar's office. The typical student load is four courses. The staff of the Registrar's office then enters the students' forms into the mainframe computer system. Once the students' curriculum for the semester has been entered, a batch job is run overnight to assign students to courses. Most of the time the students get their first choice; however, in those cases where there is a conflict, the Registrar's office talks with each student to get additional choices. Once all the students have been successfully assigned to courses, a hard copy of the students' schedule is sent to the students for their verification. Most student registrations are processed within a week, but some exceptional cases take up to two weeks to solve.

Once the initial registration period is completed, professors receive a student roster for each course they are scheduled to teach.

RISKS FOR THE COURSE REGISTRATION PROBLEM

THE DEVELOPMENT TEAM identified that the major risk to the system involved the ability to store and access the curriculum information efficiently. They developed several prototypes that evaluated data storage and access mechanisms for each database management system under consideration. The results of the prototypes led to the decision that the database risk could be mitigated. Additional prototypes were also developed to study the hardware needs for the university as a result of moving to an online registration system.

ESU COURSE REGISTRATION PROBLEM STATEMENT

AT THE BEGINNING of each semester, students may request a course catalog containing a list of course offerings for the semester. Information about each course, such as professor, department, and prerequisites, will be included to help students make informed decisions.

The new system will allow students to select four course offerings for the coming semester. In addition, each student will indicate two alternative choices in case a course offering becomes filled or canceled. No course offering will have more than ten students or fewer than three students. A course offering with fewer than three students will be canceled. Once the registration process is completed for a student, the registration system sends information to the billing system so the student can be billed for the semester.

Professors must be able to access the online system to indicate which courses they will be teaching, and to see which students signed up for their course offerings.

For each semester, there is a period of time during which students can change their schedule. Students must be able to access the system during this time to add or drop courses.

SUMMARY

THE INCEPTION PHASE is a discovery phase. The problem to be solved is verbalized and discussed among the team and with customers. Assumptions are expressed and may be verified or rejected using proof of concept prototyping techniques. The output of this phase is the identification of the external interfaces, an initial risk assessment, and a set of system requirements. Customers, clients, users, and other interested parties bring various ideas and points of view to this phase and offer the possibility of an early and enthusiastic buy-in.

The Use Case Model

THE FUNCTIONAL REQUIREMENTS of a system under development (i.e., the functionality that must be provided by the system) are documented in a use case model that illustrates the system's intended functions (use cases), its surroundings (actors), and relationships between the use cases and actors (use case diagrams). At the same time, it is useful to see the flow of control and the flow of data between the different scenarios represented in a use case. Activity diagrams are used to visually document the different flows in a use case.

SYSTEM BEHAVIOR

A.3.1

THE MOST IMPORTANT role of a use case model is one of communication. It provides a vehicle used by the customers or end users and the developers to discuss the system's functionality and behavior. The use case model starts in the Inception phase with the identification of actors and principal use cases for the system. The model is then matured in the Elaboration phase—more detailed information is added to the identified use cases, and additional use cases are added on an as-needed basis.

CREATING THE USE CASE MODEL

1. Right-click on the owning project in the Model Explorer and select New > UML Model.
2. Select Use Case Model.
3. Accept the default name of Use Case Model.
4. Click Finish.

This will add a use case model as shown in Figure 3-1.

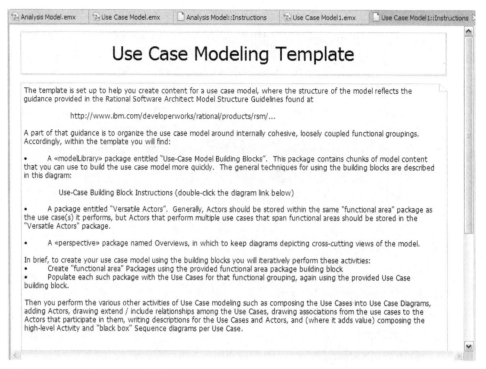

Figure 3-1   Use Case Model

Use Case Model Template

A.3.2

IBM Rational Software Architect uses a model template when a new use case model is created. The template contains model elements that can be used to help you structure your model:

- Overviews package

- Use-Case Building Blocks package

- Versatile Actors package

The Overviews package contains two default diagrams that are used to provide an overview of the system. The Actors overview is a visualization of the actors in the model. For small models, it could contain all of the actors in the model. For larger models, it may contain only some of the actors. The Context Overview diagram shows the "most important" use cases in your model. Again, for a small model this may be all of the use cases. For larger models, this diagram usually contains the architecturally significant use cases.

The Use-Case Building Blocks package contains model elements that can be copied to the use case model, allowing you to create model elements for your own use. The first element is a package called ${functional.area}, and this package contains a use case diagram. If you have a large model, you may want to group your use cases into functional areas. This is when you would use this building block. Grouping use cases into functional areas for smaller models is probably overkill. The second model element is called ${use.case}, which is a prototypical use case containing optional activity and sequence diagrams. This model element can be used for all types of models. The nice part of using this building block is that the entire structure for a use case (use case, activity diagram, and sequence diagrams) will automatically be created for you.

Sometimes an actor may communicate with use cases that are in different functional areas. That is where the Versatile Actors package comes into play since it contains those actors. This package contains one use case diagram that shows all of the actors that communicate with use cases that cross functional boundaries.

Functional Areas Packages

For the Course Registration System we have two functional areas: Course Registration and System Maintenance.

CREATING FUNCTIONAL AREA PACKAGES

1. Click Ctrl and drag the ${functional.area} package to the desired model location (in our case, we will drag it to the Use Case Model).

2. Right-click on ${functional.area} and select Find/
   Replace. . . .
3. Enter ${functional.area} in the Find what: field.
4. Click Replace >>. *Replace ALL*
5. Enter the name of the functional area in the Replace
   field.
6. Click OK.

The name of the package as well as the name of the use case
diagram in the package will be replaced. The functional areas
for the Course Registration System are shown in Figure 3-2.

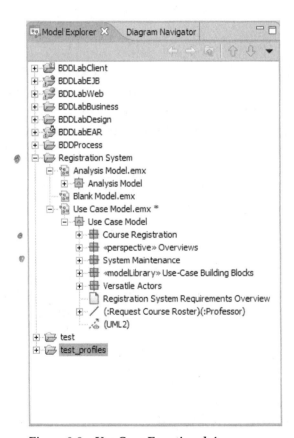

Figure 3-2   Use Case Functional Areas

ACTORS

ACTORS ARE NOT part of the system—they represent anyone or anything that must interact with the system. An actor may:

- Only input information to the system
- Only receive information from the system
- Input and receive information to and from the system

Typically, these actors are found in the problem statement and by conversations with customers and domain experts. The following questions may be used to help identify the actors for a system:

- Who is interested in a certain requirement?
- Where in the organization is the system used?
- Who will benefit from the use of the system?
- Who will supply the system with this information, use this information, and remove this information?
- Who will support and maintain the system?
- Does the system use an external resource?
- Does one person play several different roles?
- Do several people play the same role?
- Does the system interact with a legacy system?

In the UML, an actor is represented as a stickman. In IBM Rational Software Architect and IBM Rational Software Modeler, an actor is represented by the person icon shown in Figure 3-3.

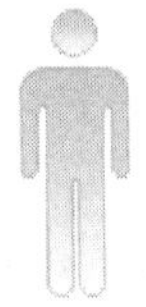

Actor1

Figure 3-3   Actor in Rational Software Architect

What Constitutes a "Good" Actor?

Care must be taken when identifying the actors for a system. This identification is done in an iterative fashion—the first cut at the list of actors for a system is rarely the final list. For example, is a new student a different actor than a returning student? Suppose you initially say the answer to this question is yes. The next step is to identify how the actor interacts with the system. If the new student uses the system differently than the returning student, they are different actors. If they use the system in the same way, they are the same actor. Another example is the creation of an actor for every role a person may play. This may also be overkill. A good example is a teaching assistant in the ESU Course Registration System. The teaching assistant takes classes and teaches classes. The capabilities needed to select courses to take and to teach are already captured by the identification of functionality needed by the Student and the Professor actors. Therefore, there is no need for a Teaching Assistant actor. By looking at the identified actors and documenting how they use the system, you will iteratively arrive at a good set of actors for the system.

Actors in the ESU Course Registration System

The previous questions were answered as follows:

■   Students want to browse the course catalog and register for courses.

- Professors want to select courses to teach and request a course roster.

- The Registrar must create the curriculum and generate a catalog for the semester.

- The Registrar must maintain all the information about courses, professors, and students.

- The Billing System must receive billing information from the system.

Based on the answers to the questions posed, the following actors have been identified: Student, Professor, Registrar, and the Billing System. Since the Student and the Billing System only deal with course registration, we will locate them in the Course Registration package. Likewise, the Registrar only deals with curriculum maintenance, so we will add the Registrar to the System Maintenance package. The Professor is a different story. The Professor wants to request a course roster, which belongs to the Course Registration package, and the Professor also needs to select courses to teach, which belongs to the System Maintenance package. Since this actor interacts with use cases in different functional areas, we will add it to the Versatile Actors package.

CREATING ACTORS

1. Right-click on the owning package in the Model Explorer and select Add UML > Actor.
2. While the new actor is still selected, enter its name.

The actors for the ESU Course Registration System are shown in Figure 3-4.

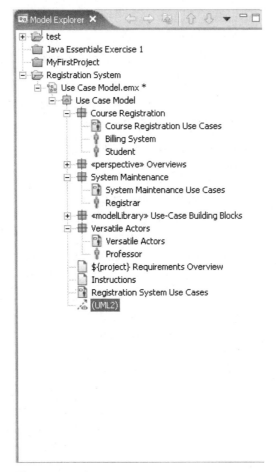

Figure 3-4   Actors

Documenting Actors

A brief description for each actor should be added to the model. The description should identify the role the actor plays while interacting with the system.

The actor descriptions for the ESU Course Registration System are as follows:

- Student—a person who is registered to take classes at the university

- Professor—a person who is certified to teach classes at the university

- Registrar—the person who is responsible for the maintenance of the ESU Course Registration System

- Billing System—the external system responsible for student billing

DOCUMENTING ACTORS

1. Click to select the actor in the Model Explorer.
2. Select the Properties tab. If this tab is not visible, select Window > Show View > Properties to make it visible.
3. Select Documentation.
4. Enter the description for the actor.

The documentation for the Student actor is shown in Figure 3-5.

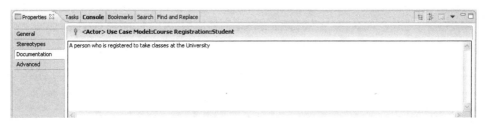

Figure 3-5   Student Actor Documentation

USE CASES

USE CASES MODEL a dialogue between an actor and the system. They represent the functionality provided by the system, that is, what capabilities will be provided to an actor by the system. The collection of use cases for a system constitutes all the defined ways the system may be used. The formal definition for a use case is as follows:

> A use case is a sequence of transactions performed by a system that yields a measurable result of values for a particular actor.

The following questions may be used to help identify the use cases for a system:

- What are the tasks of each actor?

- Will any actor create, store, change, remove, or read information in the system?

- What use case will create, store, change, remove, or read this information?

- Will any actor need to inform the system about sudden, external changes?

- Does any actor need to be informed about certain occurrences in the system?

- What use cases will support and maintain the system?

- Can all functional requirements be performed by the use cases?

In the UML, a use case is represented as an oval, as shown in Figure 3-6.

UseCase1

Figure 3-6   The UML Representation of a Use Case

What Constitutes a "Good" Use Case?

Over the years there has been a lot of discussion dealing with the "goodness" of a use case. One problem that I have encountered is the level of detail found in use cases. That is, how big (or how little) should they be? There is no one, right answer. The rule of thumb that I apply is the following:

- A use case typically represents a major piece of functionality that is complete from beginning to end.

- A use case must deliver something of value to an actor.

For example, in the ESU Course Registration System, the student must select the courses for a semester, the student must be added to the course offerings, and the student must be billed. Is this three use cases, or just one? I would make it one because the functionality represents what happens from beginning to end. What good would the system be if a student was not added to the courses selected (or at least notified if the addition does not occur)? Or if the student was not billed? (The university would not stay in business if all courses were free!)

Another problem is how to bundle functionality that is different but seems to belong together. For example, the Registrar must add courses, delete courses, and modify courses. Three use cases or one use case? Here again, I would make this one use case—the maintenance of the curriculum, since the functionality is started by the same actor (the Registrar) and deals with the same entities in the system (the curriculum).

If you are not careful, you may fall into the world of functional decomposition. One way to avoid this is to treat your use cases in the following ways:

- Determine if the use cases represent something that shows start-to-finish functionality that is needed by the actor initiating the use case.

- Avoid "small" use cases—use cases that provide one piece of functionality.

- Avoid "many" use cases. I have found that very complicated systems will typically have at most 50 use cases.

- Avoid use cases whose name implies one piece of functionality. For example, Enter Professor ID would not be a good use case for our system.

Use Cases in the ESU Course Registration System

The following needs must be addressed by the system:

- The Student actor needs to use the system to browse the course catalog and register for courses.

- After the course selection process is completed, the Billing System must be supplied with billing information.

- The Professor actor needs to use the system to select the courses to teach for a semester, and must be able to receive a course roster from the system.

- The Registrar is responsible for the generation of the course catalog for a semester, and for the maintenance of all information about the curriculum, the students, and the professors needed by the system.

Based on these needs, the following use cases have been identified:

- Register for courses
- Browse course catalog
- Select courses to teach
- Request course roster
- Maintain course information
- Maintain professor information
- Maintain student information
- Create course catalog

CREATING USE CASES

1. Right-click on ${use.case} in the Use-Case Building Blocks package and select Copy.
2. Right-click on the functional area package for the new use case and select Paste.
3. Right-click on ${use.case} and select Find/Replace. . . .
4. Enter ${use.case} in the Find what: field.
5. Click Replace > >.
6. Enter the name of the use case in the Replace field.
7. Click OK.

The identified use cases for the Course Registration System are shown in Figure 3-7.

Documenting Use Cases

Just showing the graphical notation for a use case is not enough. Each use case is accompanied by text explaining the purpose of the use case as well as what functionality is accomplished when the use case executes.

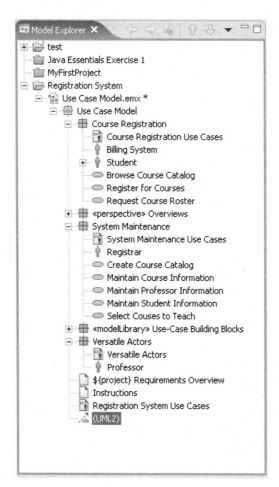

Figure 3-7   Use Cases

The Use Case Specification

The use case specification should include the following:

- Brief description of the use case that states the purpose of the use case in a few sentences, providing a high-level definition of the functionality provided by the use case

- When and how the use case starts and ends
- What interaction the use case has with the actors
- What data is needed by the use case
- What data is produced by the use case
- Flow of events written in terms of what the system should do, not how the system does it
- The normal sequence of events for the use case, typically called the basic flow of events
- Description of any alternate or exceptional flows
- Use case preconditions (what has to occur before the use case starts)
- Use case postconditions (what occurs after the use case ends)
- Extension points (use cases that may extend the basic use case with optional behavor)

The use case specification is typically created in the Elaboration phase in an iterative manner. At first, only a brief description of the steps needed to carry out the normal flow of the use case (i.e., what functionality is provided by the use case) is written. As analysis progresses, the steps are fleshed out to add more detail. Finally, the exceptional flows are added to the use case (the what happens if . . . part of the flow of events).

Each project should use a standard template for the creation of the use case specification. I use the template from the Rational Unified Process:

1.0 Use Case Name

    1.1 Brief Description

2.0 Flow of Events

    2.1 Basic Flow

2.2 Alternate Flows

2.2.x < Alternate Flow x >

3.0 Special Requirements

3.x < Special Requirement x >

4.0 Preconditions

4.x < Precondition x >

5.0 Post Conditions

5.x < Postcondition x >

6.0 Extension Points

6.x < Extension Point x >

A sample completed use case specification document for the Browse Course Catalog use case follows.

1.   Use Case Name

Browse Course Catalog

1.1 Brief Description

This use case is started by the Student. It provides the capability for the student to view the courses and their course offerings for a specified semester.

2.   Flow of Events

2.1 Basic Flow

2.1.1 BROWSE CATALOG

The use case begins when the student chooses to browse the course catalog.

2.1.2 BROWSE BY SUBJECT AREA

The system displays the functions available to the student. The functions are Browse by Subject Area, Search for a Course Offering, or Quit. The student selects Browse by Subject Area.

2.1.3 SELECT SUBJECT AREA

The system displays the list of subject areas to the student. The student selects a subject area.

2.1.4 DISPLAY COURSE OFFERINGS

The system displays the list of course offerings to the student. The student selects a course offering. The system retrieves and displays the course offering details: Course Offering Name, Course Offering Number, Location, Day(s), Time, Professor, and Prerequisite Courses. The use case ends.

2.2 Alternative Flows

2.2.1 SEARCH FOR A COURSE OFFERING

At BF BROWSE BY SUBJECT AREA, the student selects Search for a Course Offering. The student enters the course offering number. The system retrieves and displays the course offering details: Course Offering Name, Course Offering Number, Day(s), Time, Professor, and Prerequisite Courses. The use case ends.

2.2.2 QUIT

The student can quit any time during the use case. When the student selects the Quit option, the use case ends.

2.2.3 CANNOT RETRIEVE COURSE OFFERING INFORMATION

At BF DISPLAY COURSE OFFERINGS or AF SEARCH FOR A COURSE OFFERING, the system determines that the Course Catalog is not available. The system displays an error message and the use case ends.

3.   Special Requirements
     None.

4.   Preconditions
     Course Catalog must exist.

5.   Post Conditions
     None

6.   Extension Points
     None

You can create a use case specification using any word processor, but if you use IBM Rational RequisitePro, there is very tight integration with IBM Rational Software Architect.

LINKING TO AN IBM RATIONAL REQUISITE-PRO PROJECT

1.   Select Window > Show View > Requirement Explorer.
2.   Click the Open RequisitePro project button (you must create a project in RequisitePro first).
3.   Navigate to the directory containing the RequisitePro project.
4.   Select the project.
5.   Click Open.

CREATING USE CASE DATABASE REQUIREMENTS

1.   Select the use case in the Model Explorer.
2.   Drag the use case onto the Use Cases package in the Requirement Explorer.

Use case requirements are shown in Figure 3-8.

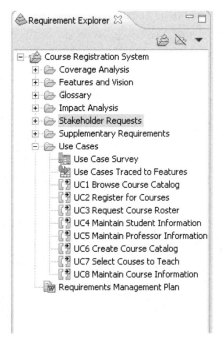

Figure 3-8   Use Case Requirements

Once the use case requirements are created, you can switch to IBM Rational RequisitePro to enter the rest of the use case specification text.

SELECTING REQUIREMENTS IN IBM RATIONAL REQUISITE PRO

1. Right-click on the use case requirement in the Requirement Explorer.
2. Select Select Requirement in > RequisitePro.

A use case specification document should be created in Rational RequisitePro. The use case requirement can be moved into the document. The rest of the text for the use case specification is added to the use case specification document. Each "part" of the use case specification should be a child requirement of the use case requirement. The use case specification document for the Browse Course Catalog use case is shown in Figure 3-9.

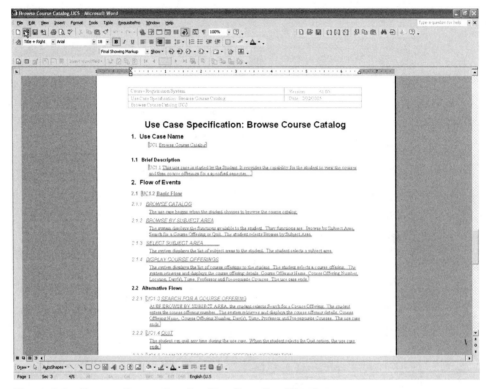

Figure 3-9   Browse Course Catalog Use Case Specification

Once all of the child requirements are created, they can be viewed in the Requirement Explorer.

VIEWING CHILD REQUIREMENTS

1. Right-click in the Requirement Explorer.
2. Select Refresh.

The child requirements for the Browse Course Catalog use case are shown in Figure 3-10.

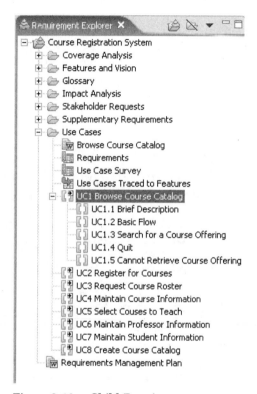

Figure 3-10   Child Requirements

USE CASE DIAGRAMS

A USE CASE diagram is used to visualize the relationships between use cases and actors and between use cases and other use cases. The UML does not specify how many use case diagrams to create—you just create as many as you need to communication the functional requirements of the system (and typically, the more use cases in the system, the more diagrams you will probably create). However, I have found that no matter how many use cases you have, the following use case diagrams are always created:

- Main use case diagram showing the functional use case packages

- A diagram showing the most important use cases (for smaller systems this diagram may contain all of the use cases; for larger systems this diagram contains the architecturally significant use cases)

- A main diagram for each functional area showing the use cases in that functional area

If you used the use case model template, all of these diagrams are created—all you need to do is populate them.

OPENING A USE CASE DIAGRAM

1. In the Model Explorer, double-click on the diagram.

You may feel the need to create additional diagrams. This is usually the case if you have a large system with many use cases. Some examples of additional diagrams are:

- A diagram showing all of the use cases for a given actor

- A diagram showing use cases that are executed in one sequence

- Use cases that are being implemented for a particular iteration

CREATING A USE CASE DIAGRAM

1. In the Model Explorer, right-click on the owning package.

2. Select Add Diagram > Use Case.

3. This will add a new diagram to the Model Explorer. While the diagram is still selected, enter its name.

Actor–Use Case Relationships

Communication between an actor and a use case is shown with an association. This type of association is often referred to as a *communicate association*. There is only one communicate association between an actor and a use case no matter how many messages pass between the actor and the use case.

CREATING USE CASE–ACTOR RELATIONSHIPS

1. Double-click on the diagram containing the relationship to open it.

2. Drag the use case from the Model Explorer onto the diagram.

3. Select the actor(s) that interact with the use case (Note: to multi-select actors in the Model Explorer, depress the Shift key) and drag them onto the diagram.

4. Click the Association item in the Palette.

5. Click on the actor in the diagram and drag the association to the use case.

The use case diagrams for the Course Registration System are shown in Figures 3-11, 3-12, 3-13, and 3-14.

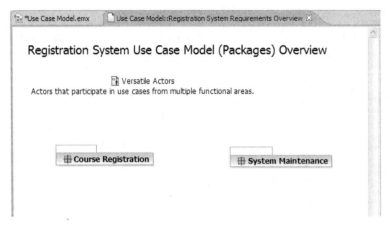

Figure 3-11   Overview Diagram

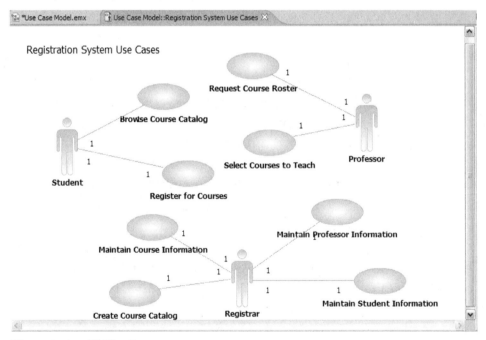

Figure 3-12   All Use Cases

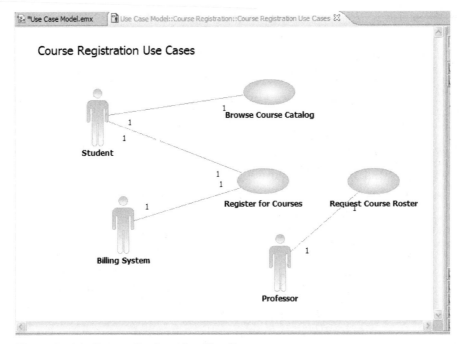

Figure 3-13   Course Registration Use Cases

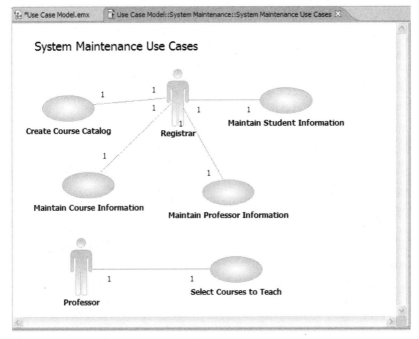

Figure 3-14   System Maintenance Use Cases

Relationships Between Use Cases

There are two types of relationships that may exist between use cases: include and extend. Multiple use cases may share pieces of the same functionality. This functionality is placed in a separate use case rather than documenting it in every use case that needs it.

Include relationships are created between the new use case and any other use case that "uses" its functionality. For example, each use case in the ESU Course Registration System starts with the verification of the user. This functionality can be captured in a User Verification use case, which is then used by other use cases as needed. An include relationship is drawn as a dependency relationship that points from the base use case to the used use case.

An extend relationship is used to show

- Optional behavior

- Behavior that is run only under certain conditions, such as triggering an alarm

- Several different flows that may be run based on actor selection

For example, if a current selection is not available during the Register for Courses use cases, the student may want to see what other courses are available. Thus, the Browse Course Catalog use case may be an extension of the Register for Courses use case. An *extend* relationship is drawn as a dependency relationship that points from the extension to the base use case.

The UML has a concept called a stereotype, which provides the capability of extending the basic modeling elements to create new elements. Thus, the concept of a stereotype allows the UML to have a minimal set of symbols that may be extended where needed to provide the communication artifacts that have meaning for the system under development. Stereotype names are included within guillemets (< < > >) and placed along the relationship line. Stereotypes are used to create the needed use case relationships. The stereotype < < communicate > > may be added to an association to show that the association is a communicate association. This is optional since an association is the only type of relationship allowed between an actor and a use case. Include and extend relationships must use stereotypes since they are both represented by a dependency relationship.

CREATING INCLUDE AND EXTEND RELATIONSHIPS

1. Drag the use cases in the relationship from the Model Explorer onto a diagram.
2. Select the Include or Extend icon in the Palette. (The last used icon will be visible in the Palette. If that is not the icon that you need, click the arrow next to it to make the other relationship icons visible.)
3. For an include relationship, click on the base use case and drag the dependency relationship to the included use case.
4. For an extend relationship, click on the use case with the extended functionality and drag the relationship to the base use case.

Use case relationships are shown in Figure 3-15.

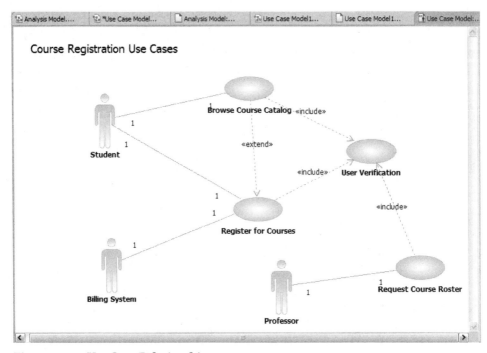

Figure 3-15   Use Case Relationships

ACTIVITY DIAGRAMS

A.3.3

ACTIVITY DIAGRAMS MAY be created at this stage in the life cycle to show the flow of control and data flow within a use case. Activities are containing nodes that include actions and control flow and/or data flow between the actions. The diagrams show action sequence, control flows, and joins and decision points.

Actions

An action represents the performance of some behavior in the workflow. In UML, an action is shown as a round-cornered rectangle, as shown in Figure 3-16.

Actions can be determined by examining the use case specification and determining what behaviors are needed to

Figure 3-16   Action

execute the steps of the use case. Many times, the titles created for a use case requirement will map to a behavior that a use case must execute

CREATING ACTIONS

1. Click to select the Action icon from the Palette.
2. Click on the activity diagram window to place the action.
3. While the action is still selected, enter the name of the action.

Control Flows

Once an action finishes, control is passed to the next action in the activity diagram. Control flows show the passing of control from one action to the next action in sequence. In UML, a control flow is represented as a directed arrow, as shown in Figure 3-17.

Figure 3-17   Control Flow

CREATING CONTROL FLOWS

1. Click to select the Control Flow icon from the Palette.
2. Click on the originating action and drag the control flow arrow to the successor action.

Decision Points

When modeling the workflow of a system, it is often necessary to show where the flow of control branches based on a decision point. The control flows from a decision point contain a guard condition, which is used to determine which path from the decision point is taken. Decisions, along with their guard conditions, allow you to show alternate paths through a workflow. In UML, a decision point is shown as a diamond, and the guard conditions are shown within square brackets, as shown in Figure 3-18.

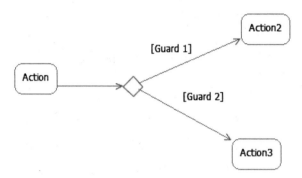

Figure 3-18   Decision Point

CREATING DECISION POINTS

1. Click to select the Decision icon from the Palette.
2. Click on the activity diagram window to place the decision.
3. While the decision is still selected, enter the name of the decision.
4. Click to select the Control Flow icon on the Palette.
5. Click on the originating activity and drag the transition to the Decision icon.

CREATING GUARD CONDITIONS

1. Click to select the control flow in the diagram.
2. Select the Properties window.
3. Enter the guard condition in the Body Text field.

Object Flows

There are many times that you want to show the flow of data along with the flow of control—that is, the data that flows between actions. An object flow denotes the flow from an action to data or from data to an action. In UML, data is typically shown as a rectangle, and like a control flow, a data flow is shown as a directed arrow. Flow of data is shown in Figure 3-19.

Figure 3-19   Data Flow

CREATING DATA STORES AND OBJECT FLOWS

1. Click to select the Object Node icon from the palette.
2. Click on the activity diagram window and select Create New Datastore Node.
3. While the data store is still selected, enter the name of the data store.
4. Click to select the Object Flow icon on the Palette.
5. Click on the originating action and drag the object flow to the data store.

Forking and Joining Flows of Control

In a workflow there are typically some actions that may be done in parallel. A fork node allows you to specify what activities may be done concurrently. A join node is used to show joins in the workflow—that is, what actions must complete before processing may continue. That said, a fork node has one incoming control flow and many outgoing control flows. A join node has many incoming control flows and one outgoing control flow. In UML, fork and join nodes are shown as line segments, as shown in Figure 3-20.

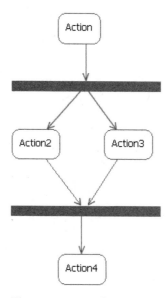

Figure 3-20   Fork and Join Nodes

CREATING FORK NODES OR JOIN NODES

1. Click the arrow next to the Control Node icon in the Palette.

2. Select Fork or Join.

3. Click on the activity diagram window to place the fork node or join node.

4. Resize as needed.

Activity Partitions

Activity partitions may be used to group actions with something in common in an activity diagram. This typically is done to show what person or organization is responsible for the activities contained in the partition. Activity partitions are shown in Figure 3-21.

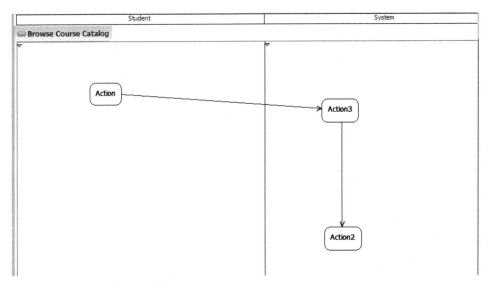

Figure 3-21   Activity Partitions

CREATING ACTIVITY PARTITIONS

1. Right-click on the activity diagram in the Model Explorer.

2. Select Add UML > Partition.

3. While the partition is still selected in the Model Explorer, add its name.

Initial and Final Nodes

There are special symbols that are used to show the starting and final nodes in a workflow. The starting node is shown using a solid filled circle, and the final nodes are shown using a bull's eye. There is one starting node for the activity and there may be more than one ending node (one for each alternate flow in the activity). Initial and final nodes are shown in Figure 3-22.

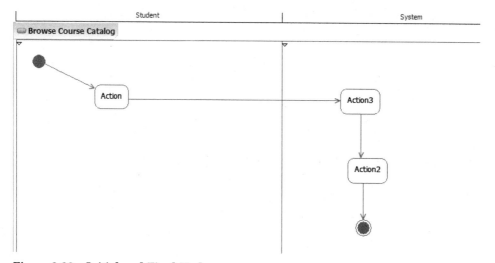

Figure 3-22   Initial and Final Nodes

CREATING INITIAL AND FINAL NODES

1. Click to select the Initial or the Activity Final icon from the Palette.

2. Click on the activity diagram window to place the initial or final node.

3. If you added an initial node, click on the Control Flow icon in the Palette, click on the initial node, and drag the control flow to the first action in the activity.

4. If you added a final node, click on the Control Flow icon in the Palette, click on the successor action, and drag the control flow to the final node.

The activity diagram for the Browse Course Catalog use case is shown in Figure 3-23.

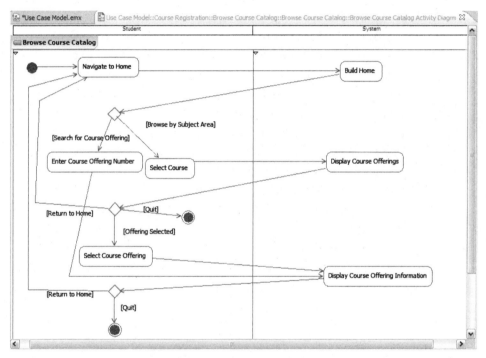

Figure 3-23   Browse Course Catalog Activity Diagram

SUMMARY

SYSTEM BEHAVIOR IS documented in a use case model that illustrates the system's intended functions (use cases), its surroundings (actors), and the relationships between the use cases and actors (use case diagrams).

The most important role of a use case model is to communicate the system's functionality and behavior to the customer or end user.

Actors are not part of the system—they represent anyone or anything that must interact with the system under development.

Use cases represent the functionality provided by the system. They model a dialogue between an actor and the system.

Each use case contains a flow of events, which is a description of the events needed to accomplish the use case functionality. The flow of events is written in terms of *what* the system should do, not *how* the system does it.

A use case diagram is a graphical representation of some or all of the actors, use cases, and their interactions for a system.

There are two types of use case relationships: include and extend. An include relationship is drawn to show functionality that is shared by several use cases; an extend relationship depicts optional behavior of a use case.

T.3.1

Activity diagrams represent the dynamics of the system. They are flow charts that are used to show the workflow of a system. At this point in the life cycle, activity diagrams may be created to represent the flow within a use case.

DEVELOPERWORKS LINKS

A.3.1 Gottesdiener, E. Use case best practices. IBM developerWorks, November 2003: http://www-128.ibm.com/developerworks/rational/library/344.html

A.3.2 Pan-Wei Ng. Adopting use cases. developerWorks, November 2003: http://www-128.ibm.com/developerworks/rational/library/1809.html

A.3.3   Ericcson, M. Activity diagrams: What they are and
        how to use them. developerWorks, April 2004:
        http://www128.ibm.com/developerworks/rational/
        library/2802.html

T.3.1   Two-part use case modeling Web-based course
        (fee-based): Principles of use case modeling with
        UML. developerWorks, January 2005. Part One
        begins at http://www-128.ibm.com/developerworks/
        rational/library/4177.html

The Analysis Model

AN ANALYSIS MODEL is the first step down the path of system implementation. With the analysis model you are concerned with "how" the system will be implemented. An analysis model may be a temporary artifact that is matured into the design model as analysis and design progress or it may be a living artifact that provides a non-implementation-specific view of the system. Some reasons for maintaining a separate analysis model are as follows:

- The system must be designed for multiple target environments, with separate design architectures. In this case, the analysis model is a platform-independent model that can be transformed into multiple platform-specific models. This is the idea expressed in the Object Management Group's (OMG) Model Driven Architecture initiative.

- The design is complex, such that a simplified, abstracted "design" is needed to introduce the design to new team members.

If you decide to maintain separate analysis and design models, you will need to take the time to make sure the models remain consistent.

CREATING AN ANALYSIS MODEL

A.4.1   CREATING AN ANALYSIS model in IBM Rational Software Architect is simple and straightforward.

CREATING THE ANALYSIS MODEL
1. Right-click on the owning project in the Model Explorer and select New > UML Model.
2. Select Analysis Model. _No, choose_
   "Rup Analysis Model"

3. Accept the default name of Analysis Model.
4. Click Finish.

This will add an analysis model as shown in Figure 4-1.

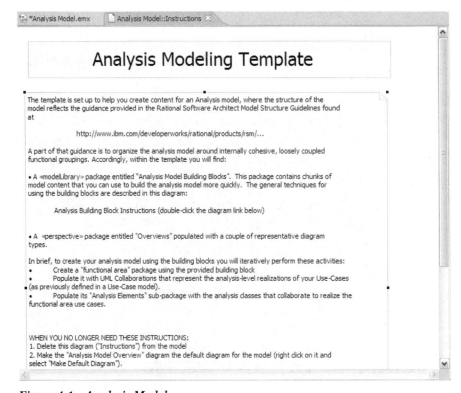

Figure 4-1   Analysis Model

ANALYSIS MODEL TEMPLATE

IBM RATIONAL SOFTWARE ARCHITECT uses a model template when a new analysis model is created. The template contains model elements that can be used to help you structure your model:

- Overviews package
- Analysis Building Blocks package

The Overviews package contains four default diagrams that are used to provide an overview of the system. The Domain Model diagram shows all analysis classes with an analysis stereotype of < <entity> >. These classes are typically "things" that need to be manipulated to realize the functionality of the system. The Key Abstractions diagram shows the significant analysis classes in the system. These classes are usually the classes that will help define the system architecture. The Key Controllers diagram shows all classes with the stereotype of < <control> >. These classes typically manage the sequence of messages in a use case. Finally, the UI diagram shows all of the classes with a stereotype of < <boundary> that reflect an interface to a human actor. These classes are used to drive the user interface design of the system.

The Analysis Building Blocks package contains model elements that can be copied to the analysis model, enabling you to create model elements for your own use. The first element is a package called ${functional.area}, and this package contains a class diagram. If you have a large model, you may want to group your analysis classes into functional areas. This is when you would use this building block. Grouping analysis classes into functional areas for smaller models is probably overkill. The second model element is called ${use.case}, which is a prototypical use case realization containing optional sequence diagrams and class diagrams. This model element can be used for all types of models. The nice part of using this building block is that the entire structure for a use case realization (use case realization, class diagram, and sequence diagrams) will automatically be created for you. Finally, there are three classes that can be used to create entity, control, and boundary classes.

Functional Area Packages

For the Course Registration System we will create two functional areas that correspond to the functional areas defined in the use case model: Course Registration and System Maintenance.

CREATING FUNCTIONAL AREA PACKAGES

1. Click Ctrl and drag the ${functional.area} package to the desired model location (in our case, we will drag it to the Analysis model). This will create a copy of the ${functional.area} template for your own use.
2. Right-click on ${functional.area} and select Find/Replace...
3. Enter ${functional.area} in the Find what: field.
4. Click Replace > >.
5. Enter the name of the functional area in the Replace field.
6. Click OK.

The name of the package as well as the name of the class diagram in the package will be replaced. The functional areas for the Course Registration System are shown in Figure 4-2.

USE CASE REALIZATIONS

A.4.2

A USE CASE represents "what" a system should do. A use case realization represents "how" the system will perform the functionality specified in a use case. Keeping use cases separate from their realizations allows each item to be managed independently. This is really important for large systems

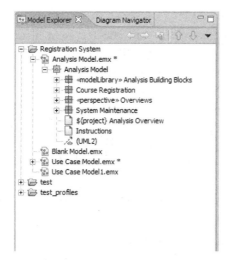

Figure 4-2   Functional Area Packages

that may have multiple implementations for the same functionality. In UML, a use case realization is represented by a
collaboration, which is drawn as a dashed oval, as shown in
Figure 4-3.

Figure 4-3   UML Notation for a Use Case Realization

During analysis, use case realizations are created for
each use case identified in the use case model. The realizations are then populated with objects belonging to analysis
classes—classes that are created to realize the functionality

specified in the use case. As the analysis model matures, most of the analysis classes will realize functionality specified by more than one use case. This is the first step in moving from the specification of the requirements to the actual implementation of the system.

CREATING A USE CASE REALIZATION

1. Press Ctrl and drag the ${use.case} package in the Analysis Building Blocks package to the desired model location (in our case, we will drag it to the appropriate functional area).
2. Right-click on ${use.case} and select Find/Replace. . . .
3. Enter ${use.case} in the Find what: field.
4. Click Replace > >.
5. Enter the name of the use case realization in the Replace field.
6. Click OK.

The name of the use case realization as well as the names of the diagrams in the use case realization will be replaced. The use case realizations for the Course Registration System are shown in Figure 4-4.

What Is an Object?

An object is a representation of an entity, either real-world or conceptual. An object can represent something concrete, such as Joe's truck or my computer, or a concept such as a chemical process, a bank transaction, a purchase order, Mary's credit history, or an interest rate.

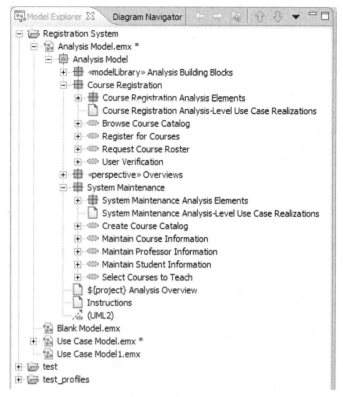

Figure 4-4   Use Case Realizations

An object is a concept, abstraction, or thing with well-defined boundaries and meaning for an application. In the UML, objects are represented as rectangles, as shown in Figure 4-5.

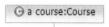

Figure 4-5   UML Notation for an Object

Each object in a system has three characteristics: state, behavior, and identity.

Object State

The state of an object is one of the possible conditions in which it may exist. The state of an object typically changes over time, and is defined by a set of properties (called attributes), with the values of the properties, plus the relationships the object may have with other objects. For example, a course offering object in the registration system may be in one of two states: *open* or *closed*. If the number of students registered for a course offering is less than ten, the state of the course offering is open. When the tenth student registers for the course offering, the state becomes closed.

Object Behavior

Behavior determines how an object responds to requests from other objects and typifies everything the object can do. Behavior is implemented by the set of operations for the object. In the registration system, a course offering could have the behaviors *add a student* and *delete a student*.

Object Identity

Identity means that each object is unique—even if its state is identical to that of another object. For example, Algebra 101, Section 1, and Algebra 101, Section 2 are two objects in the Course Registration System. Although they are both course offerings, each has a unique identity.

What Is a Class?

A class is a description of a group of objects with common properties (attributes), common behavior (operations), common relationships to other objects, and common semantics.

Thus, a class is a template to create objects. Each object is an instance of some class. For example, the CourseOffering class may be defined with the following characteristics:

- Attributes—location, time offered
- Operations—retrieve location, retrieve time of day, add a student to the offering

Algebra 101, Section 1, and Algebra 101, Section 2 are objects belonging to the CourseOffering class. Each object would have a value for the attributes and access to the operations specified by the CourseOffering class.

A good class captures one and only one abstraction—it should have one major theme. For example, a class that has the capability of maintaining information about a student and the information about all the course offerings that the student has taken over the years is not a good class since it does not have one major theme. This class should be split into two related classes: Student and StudentHistory.

Classes should be named using the vocabulary of the domain. The name should be a singular noun that best characterizes the abstraction. Acronyms may be used if the acronym has the same meaning for all involved, but if an acronym has different meanings for different people then the full name should always be used. If a class is named with an acronym, the full name should also be contained in the class documentation.

It is often hard to distinguish between an object and a class. Why is Algebra 101, Section 1 an object and not a class? What makes it different from Algebra 101, Section 2? The answers to these questions are very subjective. By looking at their structure and behavior, it can be seen that both have the same structure and behavior. They are only different course offerings for a semester. In addition, it may be noted that there are many other "things" in the Course Registration System that have the same structure and behavior (e.g., Music 101, Section1; History 101, Section 1; and History 101, Section 2). This leads to the decision to create a CourseOffering class.

In the UML, classes are represented as compartmentalized rectangles. The top compartment contains the name of the class, the middle compartment contains the structure of the class (attributes), and the bottom compartment contains the behavior of the class (operations). A class is shown in Figure 4-6.

Figure 4-6   UML Notation for a Class

Discovering Classes

A cookbook for finding classes does not exist. As Grady Booch has been known to say, "This is hard!" The IBM Rational Unified Process advocates finding the classes for a system under development by looking for boundary, control, and entity classes. These three stereotypes conform to a "model-view-controller" point of view and allow the analyst to partition the system by separating the view from the domain from the control needed by the system. Boundary, control, and entity classes are shown in Figure 4-7.

Figure 4-7   Boundary, Control, and Entity Classes

The Analysis Model template in Rational Software Architect contains Boundary, Control and Entity classes in the Analysis Building Blocks package that can be used to create boundary, control and entity classes for your model. In addition, each functional area package contains a sub-package that will contain the analysis classes for that particular functional area.

Since the analysis and design process is iterative, the list of classes will change as time moves on. The initial set of classes probably will not be the set of classes that eventually gets implemented. Thus, the term *candidate class* is often used to describe the first set of classes found for a system.

Entity Classes

An entity class models information and associated behavior that is generally long-lived. This type of class may reflect a real-world entity or it may be needed to perform tasks internal to the system. They are typically independent of their surroundings; that is, they are not sensitive to how the surroundings communicate with the system. Many times, they are application independent, meaning that they may be used in more than one application.

The first step is to examine the responsibilities documented in the flow of events for the identified use cases (i.e., what the system must do). Entity classes typically are classes that are needed by the system to accomplish some responsibility. The nouns and noun phrases used to describe the responsibility may be a good starting point. The initial list of nouns must be filtered because it could contain nouns that are outside the problem domain, nouns that are just language expressions, nouns that are redundant, and nouns that are descriptions of class structures.

Boundary Classes

Boundary classes handle the communication between the system surroundings and the inside of the system. They can provide the interface to a user or another system (i.e., the interface to an actor). They constitute the surroundings-dependent part of the system. Boundary classes are used to model the system interfaces.

Each physical actor/scenario pair is examined to discover boundary classes. The boundary classes found in the Analysis Model are typically at a high level. For example, you may model a window but not model each of its dialogue boxes and buttons. At this point, you are documenting the user interface requirements, not implementing the interface.

User interface requirements tend to be very vague—the terms *user-friendly* and *flexible* seem to be used a lot. But user-friendly means different things to different people. This is where prototyping and storyboarding techniques can be very useful. The customer can get the "look and feel" of the system and truly capture *what* user-friendly means. The *what* is then captured as the structure and behavior of the boundary class. During design these classes are refined to take into consideration the chosen user interface mechanisms—how they are to be implemented.

Boundary classes are also added to facilitate communication with other systems. During design, these classes are refined to take into consideration the chosen communication protocols.

Control Classes

Control classes model sequencing behavior specific to one or more use cases. Control classes coordinate the events needed to realize the behavior specified in the use case. You can think of a control class as "running" or "executing" the use case—they represent the dynamics of the use case. Control classes typically are application-dependent classes.

In the Analysis Model a control class is added for each use case. The control class is responsible for the flow of events in the use case.

The use of control classes is very subjective. Many authors feel that the use of control classes results in behavior being separated from data. This can happen if your control classes are not chosen wisely. If a control class is doing more than sequencing, then it is doing too much! For example, in the Course Registration System, a student selects course offerings and if the course offering is available, the student is added to it. Who knows how to add the student— the control class or the course offering? The right answer is the course offering. The control class knows when the student should be added; the course offering knows how to add the student. A bad control class would not only know when to add the student but how to add the student.

The addition of a control class per use case is only an initial cut—as analysis and design continues, control classes may be eliminated, split up, or combined.

CREATING CLASSES

1. In the Model Explorer, press Ctrl and drag the desired class (entity, control, or boundary) in the Analysis Building Blocks package to the < functional area > Analysis Elements package

2. Select the class and enter its name in the Name field in the Properties window, General section.

DOCUMENTING CLASSES

AS CLASSES ARE created, they should also be documented. The documentation should state the purpose of the class and not the structure of the class. For example, a Student class could be documented as follows: *A student is someone currently registered to take classes at the university.*

A bad definition would be the following: The name, address, and phone number of a student. This definition only tells me the structure of the class, which can be determined by looking at its attributes. It does not tell me why I need the class.

Difficulty in naming or documenting a class may be an indication that it is not a good abstraction. The following list typifies things that can happen as classes are named and documented:

- Can identify a name and a clear concise definition—good candidate class

- Can identify a name, but the definition is the same as another class—combine the classes

- Can identify a name, but need a book to document the purpose—break up the class

- Cannot identify a name or a definition—more analysis is needed to determine the correct abstractions

DOCUMENTING CLASSES

1. Select the class in the Model Explorer or on a diagram.
2. Enter the documentation in the Documentation section of the Properties window.

Finding Boundary, Control and Entity Classes in the ESU Course Registration System

Next we will look at the Browse Course Catalog use case realization. The main capability provided by this use case is enabling a student to browse the catalog of courses.

Finding Boundary Classes

The use case specification states that a student may browse the catalog by course or search for a particular course offering. We will create a boundary class called BrowseCatalog-Home to allow the student to make this decision. Since there are two different ways to browse the catalog, we will add two additional boundary classes: CourseList and CourseOfferingList. Finally, a student can choose to see the details for a particular CourseOffering, so we will create a CourseOfferingDetail boundary class.

Adding a Control Class

We are going to add a control class to manage the flow of events for this use case and we will call it CourseCatalog.

Finding Entity Classes

Our first step for finding entity classes involves looking at the nouns in the use case specification. The following nouns are found: course catalog, course, course offering, subject area, course information, and search criteria. Next, each noun is studied to see if it would make a good class. If you try to document the nouns, you usually can determine their suitability as candidate classes. Here are the definitions for the above nouns:

- Course catalog—the control class

- Course—a specific area of study in the university. Courses are organized by subject area

- Course information—details about a course (e.g., Algebra 1).

- Course offering—a course that has been allocated a specific time and location for a semester (e.g., Algebra 1, Section 1; Algebra 1, Section 2)

- Subject area—a way of categorizing courses (e.g., Mathematics)

- Search criteria—a course offering number that you want to find

Remembering the definition of an entity class and using the definitions above, we can conclude that the following classes are good candidate entity classes: Course and CourseOffering. All of the other nouns provide details about the entity classes but are not entity classes themselves.

The boundary, control, and entity classes for this use case are shown in Figure 4-8.

Our template also contains a diagram for the analysis classes for each functional area. This diagram will typically be used to visualize all of the analysis classes for a particular functional area. If there are many classes, packages may be used to group the classes.

ADDING CLASSES TO A DIAGRAM

1. Double-click on the diagram in the Model Explorer to open the diagram.
2. Select the class in the Model Explorer.
3. Drag the class onto the diagram.

The analysis classes found are shown in Figure 4-9.

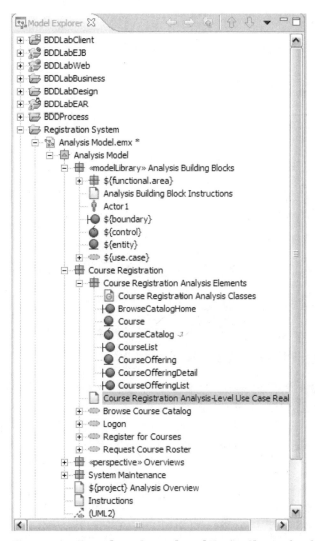

Figure 4-8   Boundary, Control, and Entity Classes for the Browse Course Catalog Use Case

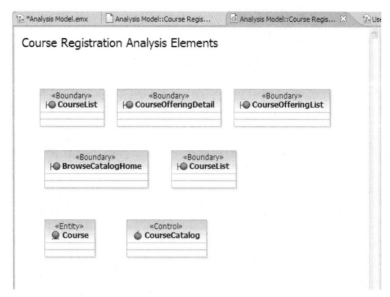

Figure 4-9   Analysis Classes

DISTRIBUTING BEHAVIOR

A.4.3

THE FUNCTIONALITY SPECIFIED in a use case is provided by distributing behavior among the analysis classes that participate in the use case realization. A sequence diagram is used to visualize the analysis classes and the messages between them that are needed to realize the functionality specified in the use case. A sequence diagram is created for the basic flow of a use case. You can also create sequence diagrams for alternate flows if you want a visualization of the alternate flow.

SEQUENCE DIAGRAMS

A.4.4

A SEQUENCE DIAGRAM shows object interactions arranged in time sequence. In the UML, an object in a sequence diagram is drawn as a rectangle containing the name of the object and its class. Each object also has its timeline, represented by a dashed line below the object. An object in a sequence diagram is shown in Figure 4-10.

Figure 4-10   UML Object in a Sequence Diagram

Messages between objects are represented by arrows that point from the client (sender of the message) to the supplier (receiver of the message).

The UML notation for objects and messages in a sequence diagram is shown in Figure 4-11.

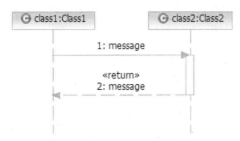

Figure 4-11   Objects and Message in a Sequence Diagram

Complexity and Sequence Diagrams

Every time I teach a class, the question "How complex can a sequence diagram be?" is always asked. The answer I always give is "Keep them simple." The beauty of these diagrams is their simplicity—it is very easy to see the objects, the object interactions, the messages between the objects, and the functionality captured by the scenario.

The next question is usually "What do I do about conditional logic?" (all the *if, then, else* logic that exists in the real world). Here, you again have a very subjective answer. If the logic is simple, involving only a few messages, I usually add the logic to one diagram and use UML fragments to visualize the conditional logic. On the other hand, if the *if, then, else* logic involves many complicated messages, I typically draw a separate diagram—one for the *if* case, one for the *then* case, and one for the *else* case. This is done to keep the diagrams simple.

Sequence diagrams can also be examined to assess the "goodness" of your object model. If you have a diagram with most of the messages coming from and going to one object (typically a control object), it may be a sign that behavior in your system is not distributed correctly. You should see messages distributed among the objects in the diagram.

Behavior in the Browse Course Catalog Use Case Realization

We will create two sequence diagrams for this use case realization—one for browse by category and one for search for a course offering since these two scenarios represent most of the functionality in the use case. The words in the use case specification will guide us in creating the sequence diagram.

CREATING A SEQUENCE DIAGRAM

1. Right-click on the owning package in the Model Explorer and select Add Diagram > Sequence Diagram.
2. While the sequence diagram is still selected, enter its name.

The Analysis Model template already contains a diagram for the basic flow and one alternate flow, so we do not have to create any new diagrams. We will use the basic flow diagram for the browse by category option and the alternate diagram for the search for a course offering option.

RENAMING A SEQUENCE DIAGRAM

1. Select the diagram in the Model Explorer.
2. Enter its new name in the Name field in the Properties window.

OPENING A SEQUENCE DIAGRAM

1. Double-click on the diagram in the Model Explorer.

The two sequence diagrams for the Browse Course Catalog use case realization are shown in Figure 4-12.

ADDING OBJECTS TO A SEQUENCE DIAGRAM

1. If the sequence diagram is not open, double-click on the diagram in the Model Explorer to open it.
2. Select the Lifeline icon in the Palette and click on the sequence diagram.
3. You can either create a lifeline from an existing element or you can create a new element. Select the appropriate choice. (In our case, we will be creating

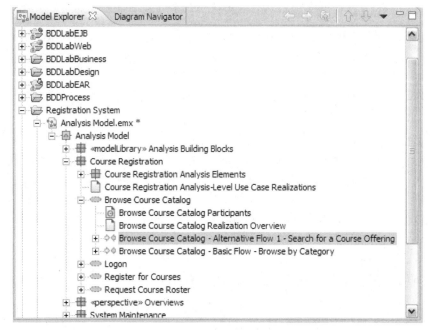

Figure 4-12   Sequence Diagrams for the Browse Course Catalog Use Case Realization

lifelines from existing elements as long as the element is in the same model. If the existing element is in another model, you need to drag the element from the Model Explorer onto the diagram.)

CREATING MESSAGES

1. Select the Synchronous Message icon from the Palette.
2. Click on the object sending the message and drag the message line to the lifeline for the object receiving the message.
3. You can either create a new operation or select an existing operation. If you choose to create a new operation, enter the new operation name.

The Browse by Category sequence diagram is shown in Figure 4-13.

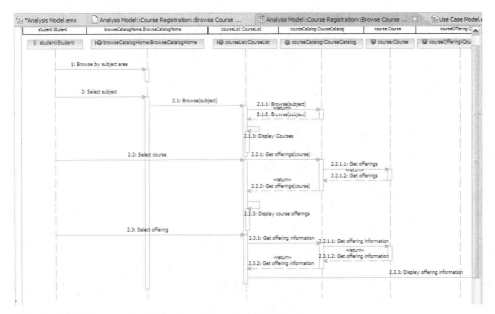

Figure 4-13   Browse by Category Sequence Diagram

UML 2.0 added a concept called a *combined fragment* to sequence diagrams. A combined fragment provides the capability to model conditional structures. Two of the more common combined fragments are Alternatives and Loops.

CREATING COMBINED FRAGMENTS

1. Select the desired Combined Fragment icon from the Palette.
2. Click on the diagram and drag the combined fragment across the lifelines and messages to be included in the combined fragment.

Two Loop combined fragments have been added to the Browse by Category sequence diagram, as shown in Figure 4-14.

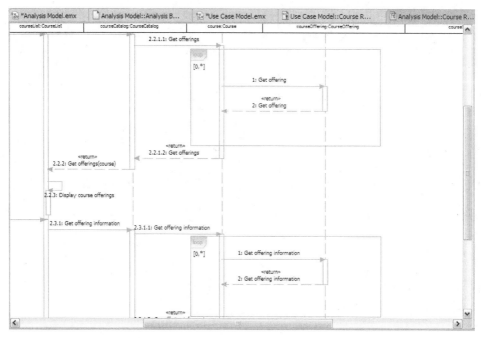

Figure 4-14   Loop Combined Fragment

Structure

The structure of an object is described by the attributes of the class. Each attribute is a data definition held by objects of the class. Objects defined for the class have a value for every attribute of the class. For example, a Course class has the attributes of name, definition, and number of credit hours. This implies that every Course object will have a value for each attribute. Attribute values do not have to be unique— there are many three-credit courses in the university.

If an object in a class does not need an attribute or operation, look at the class definition. This may be a sign that the class is not cohesive and should be broken up into separate classes. For example, suppose the CourseOffering class had the following attributes: offerNumber, location, timeOfDay, department, numberOfferingsInDepartment.

A CourseOffering may care about its department, but it probably does not care about the number of other offerings in the department. A better model would be a CourseOffering class related to a Department class. This is in keeping with the general rule that a class should have a major theme.

CREATING ATTRIBUTES

1. Right-click on the class in the Model Explorer and select Add UML > Attribute.
2. While the new attribute is still selected, enter its name.

Attributes for the Course class are shown in Figure 4-15.

VIEW OF PARTICIPATING CLASSES

A VIEW OF PARTICIPATING classes diagram shows all of the classes and their relationships for a particular use case realization. This is the diagram that we will use to create relationships between the classes. You can find the relationships by examining the sequence diagrams for the use case realization. If there is a message between two objects, then a relationship must exist between the classes. In the early stage of development we will use two types of relationships: associations and aggregations. These relationships will be refined in the design model.

An association is a bidirectional semantic connection between classes. It is not a data flow as defined in structured analysis and design—data may flow in either direction across the association. In UML, an association is shown as a solid line connecting the classes involved in the association.

An aggregation is a stronger form of association that shows a relationship between a whole and its parts. Aggregations are shown with a solid line connecting the classes involved

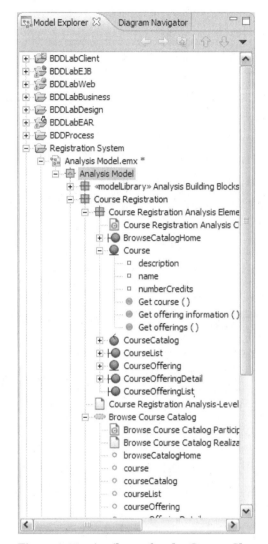

Figure 4-15   Attributes for the Course Class

in the aggreation and a diamond near the class representing the class playing the role of the "whole."

If two classes are tightly bound by a whole-part relationship, the relationship is typically an aggregation. "The decision to use aggregation is a matter of judgment and is often arbitrary. Often it is not obvious if an association should be modeled as an aggregation. If you exercise careful judgment and are consistent, the imprecise distinction between aggregation and ordinary association does not cause problems in practice."[1] A composition is a stronger form of aggregation where the part is included in at most one whole. Composite aggregation also indicates lifetime dependency—create the whole, create the part; delete the whole, delete the part.

Whether a relationship is an association or an aggregation/composition is often domain dependent. What type of relationship should be used to model a car with its tires? If the application is a service center, and the only reason you care about the tire is because it is part of the car you are servicing, then the relationship should be an aggregation. On the other hand, if the application is a tire store, you will care about the tire independent of a car, and therefore the relationship should be an association.

The UML notation for association, aggregation, and composition relationships is shown in Figure 4-16.

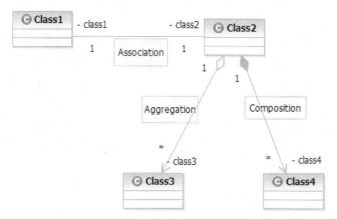

Figure 4-16   UML Notation for Association and Aggregation Relationships

1. Rumbaugh, James, et al. *Object-Oriented Modeling and Design.* Upper Saddle River, NJ: Prentice Hall, 1991, p. 58.

By examining the sequence diagrams for the Browse Course Catalog use case realization we will create the associations shown in Table 4-1.

Table 4-1   Associations for the Browse Course Catalog Use Case Realization

Class	Class
BrowseCatalogHome	CourseList
CourseList	CourseCatalog
CourseList	CourseOfferingDetail
CourseCatalog	Course

Since the relationship between a Course and a Course-Offering is a parent-child relationship where the child only exists as part of the whole, we will create a composition relationship.

The Analysis Model template has already created a class diagram to view the use case realization participants. The following tasks create the relationships between the classes.

OPENING THE BROWSE COURSE CATALOG PARTICIPANTS CLASSES DIAGRAM

1. Double-click on the diagram in the Model Explorer.

ADDING CLASSES TO A CLASS DIAGRAM

1. Click to select the class in the Model Explorer.
2. Drag it onto the diagram.

CREATING ASSOCIATIONS

1. Click on the Association icon in the Palette.

2. On a diagram, click on one class participating in the association and drag the association line to the other class participating in the association.

CREATING COMPOSITION RELATIONSHIPS

1. Click on the Composition Association icon in the Palette.
2. Click on the class playing the role of the "whole" and drag the aggregation line to the class playing the role of the "part."

The browse by category participants are shown in Figure 4-17.

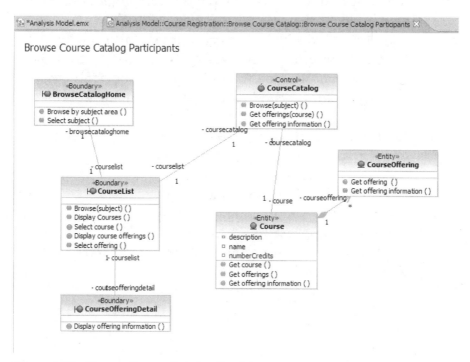

Figure 4-17   Browse Course Catalog Participants

SUMMARY

AN ANALYSIS MODEL is the first step down the path of system implementation. With an analysis model you are concerned with "how" the system will be implemented.

A use case represents "what" a system should do. A use case realization represents "how " the system will perform the functionality specified in a use case

An object is a concept, abstraction, or thing with well-defined boundaries and meaning for an application. Each object in a system has three characteristics: state, behavior, and identity.

A class is a description of a group of objects with common properties (attributes), common behavior (operations), common relationships to other objects, and common semantics. An entity class models information and associated behavior that is generally long-lived. This type of class may reflect a real-world entity or it may be needed to perform tasks internal to the system. Boundary classes handle the communication between the system surroundings and the inside of the system. They can provide the interface to a user or another system (i.e., the interface to an actor). Control classes model sequencing behavior specific to one or more use cases. Control classes coordinate the events needed to realize the behavior specified in the use case.

The functionality specified in a use case is provided by distributing behavior among the analysis classes that participate in the use case realization.

A sequence diagram shows object interactions arranged in time sequence

The structure of an object is described by the attributes of the class. Each attribute is a data definition held by objects of the class.

A view of participating classes diagram shows all of the classes and their relationships for a particular use case realization.

DEVELOPERWORKS LINKS

A.4.1 Crain, A. The simple artifacts of analysis and design. developerWorks, June 2004: http://www-128.ibm.com/developerworks/rational/library/4871.html

A.4.2 Evans, G. Getting from use cases to code (two-part series). developerWorks, July 2004. Chapter 4: http://www128.ibm.com/developerworks/rational/library/5383.html

A.4.3 Bell, D. UML basics: The class diagram. developerWorks, September 2004: http://www-128.ibm.com/developerworks/rational/library/content/RationalEdge/sep04/bell/

A.4.4 Bell, D. UML's sequence diagram. developerWorks, February 2004: http://www-128.ibm.com/developerworks/rational/library/3101.html

Chapter

5

The Design Model

- Design Model

- Design Elements

- Identifying Design Elements from Analysis Classes

- Class Diagrams

- User Interfaces

- Summary

THE DESIGN MODEL is an object model describing the realization of the analysis model, and serves as an abstraction of the implementation model and its source code. It is used to conceive as well as document the design of the software system and is essential input to activities in implementation and testing. In this chapter we'll walk you through the creation of the design model.

DESIGN MODEL

THE DESIGN MODEL can be fairly close to the implementation model, depending on how strictly you map the design model's classes, packages, and subsystems to implementation classes, files, packages, and subsystems in the implementation model. The implementation model is covered in chapter 6, but briefly it is the model that shows how the system actually looks in code. During implementation, you will often address small tactical issues related to the implementation environment that shouldn't have impact on the design model. For example, classes and subsystems can be added during implementation to handle parallel and team development.

There are no hard and fast rules on what should and should not be in the design model. The design model must define enough of the system so it can be implemented unambiguously. The level of detail will vary from project to project, system to system, and company to company. For example, for relatively simple systems like our registration system, the design may be close to a sketch, detailed only enough so that the implementer can proceed (a so-called "sketch and code" approach). Often these sketch models are considered somewhat disposable once implementation begins and starts to differ from the sketch. On the other hand, if you are modeling a complex system, the design model will be very detailed and should be maintained as the code for the system is created.

For more complex or more critical systems, the design model is the formal architecture document that is maintained and referred to for problem investigation as well as future iterations of the system.

The design may also be hierarchical or layered, such as:

- A high-level design model that sketches an overview of the overall system

- A subsystem specification model that specifies the needed interfaces and behavior of the major subsystems within the larger system

- A detailed design model for the internals of each subsystem

In any case, the design model is reviewed to ensure that all of the requirements will be satisfied once the code for the system is created.

A.5.1

In the design model, UML packages are created to organize the model. These packages contain the design elements of the system, such as design classes, interfaces, and design subsystems, that evolve from the analysis classes. Each package can contain any number of subpackages that further partition the contained design elements. These partitions normally become the architectural layers and form the basis for a second-level organization of the elements that describe the specifications and implementation details of the system.

In UML models, subsystems are a type of stereotyped component that represents independent behavioral units in a system. Looking at a subsystem from the outside, a subsystem is a single design model element that collaborates with other model elements to fulfill its responsibilities. From the inside, a subsystem is a collection of model elements that realize the interfaces and behavior of the subsystem specification. The UML notation for a subsystem is shown in Figure 5-1.

Figure 5-1   UML Notation for a Subsystem

The design model normally separates the design specifications from the design implementations. This layering helps the design by insulating the architecture from underlying implementation changes, thus making a more resilient system.

The design contract package contains the component specification package and, if desired, the design-level use case realizations. The component specification package contains the interfaces and data used to interact with the component. A design-level use case realization describes how a particular use case is realized within the design model, in terms of collaborating objects.

Within each package, the design model may contain sequence diagrams that illustrate how the objects in the classes interact, state machine diagrams that model the dynamic behavior in classes, component diagrams that describe the software architecture of the system, and deployment diagrams that describe the physical architecture of the system.

Characteristics of a Good Design Model

A good design model has the following characteristics:

- It satisfies the system requirements.

- It is resistant to changes in the implementation environment.

- It is easy to maintain in relation to other possible object models and system implementation.

- It is clear how to implement it.

- It does not include information that is best documented in program code.

- It is easily adapted to changes in requirements.

During design, the technology used to implement the solution should be identified because this decision will have impact on the design.

The Course Registration System is a relatively simple application. Therefore, we will use the simpler sketch and code approach for the design model versus the more formal document. Also, we will be using the J2EE platform for implementation as this will allow us to take advantage of various characteristices of J2EE technology and simplifying our design.

Creating a Design Model

Creating a design model in Rational Software Architect is straightforward.

CREATING THE DESIGN MODEL

1. Right-click on the owning project in the Model Explorer and select New > UML Model.
2. Select the Blank Model template.
3. Change the model file name from Blank Model to Design Model.
4. Click Finish.

This will add a design model as shown in Figure 5-2.

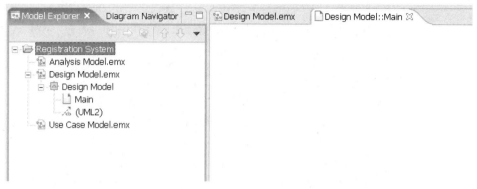

Figure 5-2   Design Model

One note here—normally for systems that will implemented in Java, we recommend using inverted Internet domain naming convention, for example, com.esu.registration.<package_name>. It is omitted here for brevity.

DESIGN ELEMENTS

ANALYSIS CLASSES REPRESENT conceptual things that can perform behavior. In design, analysis classes evolve into a number of different kinds of design elements:

- Classes, to represent a set of rather fine-grained responsibilities

- Subsystems, to represent a set of coarse-grained responsibilities, perhaps composed of a further set of subsystems, but ultimately a set of classes

- Active classes, to represent threads of control in the system

- Interfaces, to represent abstract declarations of responsibilities provided by a class or subsystem

Classes and subsystems allow us to group related responsibilities into units that can be developed in relative independence.

Subsystems are cohesive, composite building blocks that are in turn composed of classes or other subsystems. Subsystems are used to represent the work products of a development team as a single, integral unit of functionality, and as such are used both as units of control and configuration management as well as logical design elements.

An interface is a model element that defines a set of behaviors or operations offered by a class, subsystem, or component. An interface does not realize operations, it just defines them. An interface contains no attributes and therefor cannot hold data. Each interface should provide a unique and well-defined set of operations. A class, subsystem or component may realize one or more interfaces. An interface may be realized by one or more classes, subsystems, or components. The use of interfaces assists in layering your application design so that even if the actual implementation changes, the interface stays consistent (encapsulation).

As classes are identified, they should be grouped into design packages for organizational purposes. Design packages should be used primarily as a model organizational tool, to group related things together. If behavioral semantics are needed, you should use design subsystems.[1] A package should be identified for each group of classes that are functionally related. The main difference between a package and a subsystem is that a subsystem has an interface.

---

1. The semantics of "subsystem" changed in UML 2.0. Prior to UML 2.0, a subsystem was a package that exposed a number of operations. In UML 2.0 the notion of "package" was dropped from "subsystem."

When packaging boundary classes, there are two different strategies that can be applied. If it is likely that the system interface will be replaced, or undergo considerable changes, the interface should be separated from the rest of the design model. When the user interface is changed, only these packages are affected. An example of such a major change is the switch from a line-oriented interface to a window-oriented interface. If no major interface changes are planned, the boundary classes should be placed together with the entity and control classes with which they are functionally related. This way, it will be easy to see what boundary classes are affected if a certain entity or control class is changed.

A.5.2

When you start designing, you probably won't know how you want your package structure set up. Many people start with the organization used at analysis simply because it is there. You really need to look at the architecture of the system to decide upon the appropriate package structure.

CREATING DESIGN PACKAGES

1. Using the Model Explorer, right-click on the owning model and select Add UML > Package.
2. Still in the Model Explorer, give the new package a meaningful name.

Assuming the same initial structure as the analysis model, this will create design packages as shown in Figure 5-3.

As you evolve the design, it is helpful to have an overall visual view of your design model. The default diagram created when we added the design model can be used for this purpose.

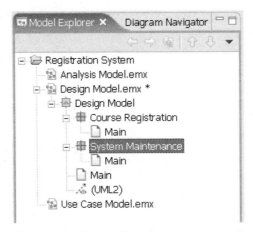

Figure 5-3   Design Packages

CREATING THE DESIGN MODEL DIAGRAM

1. Right-click on the Main diagram for the Design Model and select Refactor > Rename.

2. Enter a new name, such as Design Overview.

3. From the Model Explorer, drag and drop the design packages to the Design Model diagram visual surface.

4. If a title is desired, click the drop-down arrow next to Note in the Palette and select Text.

5. Click the mouse in the Design Model diagram visual surface where the label should appear and type the label.

This will populate the Design Model diagram as shown in Figure 5-4.

This diagram allows you to easily drill down, that is, to double-click on various packages to navigate to the lower-level packages with more detail as you evolve your design.

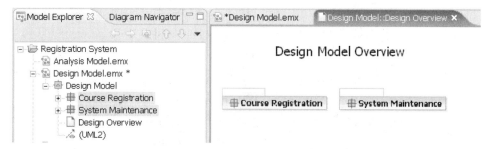

Figure 5-4   Design Model Overview Diagram

IDENTIFYING DESIGN ELEMENTS FROM ANALYSIS CLASSES

AS YOU GO through the design phase, the various analysis classes identified in the analysis phase become more concrete design elements. Analysis classes handle primarily functional requirements, and model objects from the "problem" domain, while design classes handle nonfunctional requirements, and model objects from the "solution" domain. For example, the Course analysis class represents a course offering. The Course design class might represent a class that maps the Course to a persistent data store.

An analysis class can become one or more design model elements, or a single design element may satisfy the requirements of multiple analysis classes. A few more possibilities include the following:

- An analysis class can become part of a design class in the design model.

- An analysis class can become a group of design classes that inherits from the same class in the design model.

- An analysis class can become an aggregate design class in the design model.

- An analysis class can become a group of design classes that inherits from the same class in the design model.

- An analysis class can become a group of functionally related design classes in the design model.

- An analysis class can become a design subsystem or part of a design subsystem in the design model.

- An analysis class can become a relationship in the design model.

- A relationship between analysis classes can become a design class in the design model.

As mentioned, when the analysis class is simple and already represents a single logical abstraction, it can be directly mapped, one to one, to a design class. Typically, entity classes survive relatively intact in the design model. Since entity classes are typically also persistent, that is, the data the class stores must be saved beyond the end of program execution, you should determine whether the design class should be persistent and make a note of that in the class description.

A.5.3

In our ESU Course Registration System, let's look at the analysis classes as represented in the Browse Course Catalog Participants diagram (see Figure 5-5).

There are two entity classes represented: Course and CourseOffering. It seems to make sense that both of these analysis classes should become design classes. But where should they go? Are they part of the Course Registration design package or the System Maintenance design package or somewhere else? Do they even belong in the same design package?

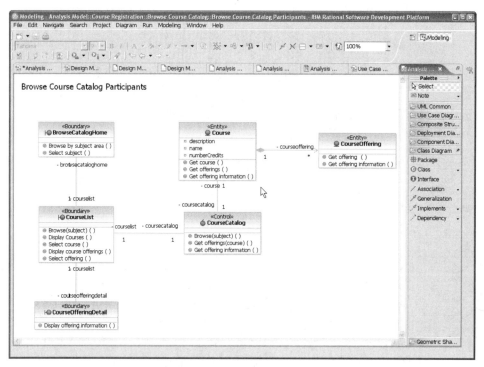

Figure 5-5   Browse Course Catalog Participants

Remember the guidelines: A package should be identi-fied for each group of classes that are *functionally* related. It seems obvious that Course and CourseOffering are func-tionally related—after all, they share the same first name. But you should always look a little deeper to make sure that things that seem related at analysis time are functionally related at design time. Some good rules of thumb:

- If changes in the behavior or structure of one class require changing another class, the two classes are functionally related. At first glance, this does not seem to be the case for Course and CourseOffering—possibly due to the simplicity of CourseOffering.

- If you delete a class, then any classes that become unnecessary are somehow connected to the deleted class. If we remove Course, then CourseOffering is really not needed. It turns out that Course and CourseOffering are functionally related and should be placed in the same design package.

- Visibility into a package can be achieved through diagrams. A good rule of thumb on diagrams is to limit them to seven classes (plus or minus two).

But which design package? Looking at the analysis model, Course and CourseOffering are used by both the Course Registration and System Maintenance analysis packages. We really don't want to tie the two together by making one depend on a package in another. This limits our flexibility for future reuse of our work. Instead, we decide to create a new package, called Course Data Objects, to hold both Course and CourseOffering (see Figure 5-6).

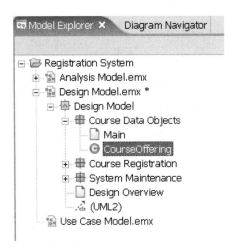

Figure 5-6   New Design Package

Now we need to create the classes in the design package. There are a number of ways to do this, and some are described here.

ADDING DESIGN CLASSES MANUALLY

1. From the Model Explorer, right-click on the package in which you want the class created and select Add UML > Class.
2. Enter the name of the class.

This will create a design class as shown in Figure 5-7.

Figure 5-7   Design Class

Another way is to work from a diagram. Right-click inside the diagram and select Add UML > Class.

CLASS DIAGRAMS

CLASS DIAGRAMS SHOW the static structure of the model, in particular, the things that exist such as classes, their internal structure, and their relationships to other classes.

A.5.4

A class diagram is displayed as a collection of model elements, such as classes, packages, and their relationships, connected as a graph to each other and to their contents.

Class diagrams may be organized into (and owned by) packages, showing only what is relevant within a particular package.

CREATING A DESIGN CLASS DIAGRAM

1. From the Model Explorer, right-click on the package in which you want the class diagram created and select Add Diagram > Class Diagram.
2. Enter the name of the diagram.

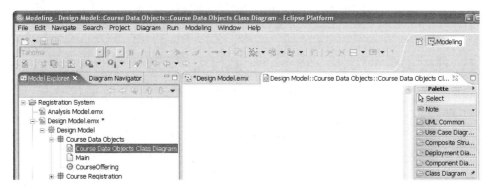

Figure 5-8   Design Class Diagram

With the design class diagram created (see Figure 5.8), design classes and attributes can be added visually. The following instructions assume the design class CourseOffering does not exist.

ADDING DESIGN CLASSES TO A CLASS DIAGRAM

1. In the class diagram, right-click and select Add UML > Class.
2. Enter the name of the class and definition (get in the habit of annotating the class at creation time).

This will create a class in the class diagram and the package, as shown in Figure 5-9.

Figure 5-9   Design Class Diagram

Attributes for the design class need to be added. For an entity class, the attributes from the analysis class usually transfer directly. But look at them to see if they still are needed as the design matures. Remember to keep the class cohesive.

ADDING ATTRIBUTES TO A DESIGN CLASS

1. Right-click on the class in the class diagram and select Add UML > Attribute.
2. Enter the attribute name.

Note that the CourseOffering analysis class had no attributes.

Operations for the design class are added. Operations are behaviors, which may affect the attributes and relationships the class holds and cause other operations to be performed. Again, a good starting point for design is the analysis model operations. But again remember to look at them to see if they still are needed as the design matures.

ADDING OPERATIONS TO A DESIGN CLASS

1. Right-click on the class in the class diagram and select Add UML > Operation.
2. Enter the operation name.

This will add an operation such as "Get offerring" to the class diagram, as shown in Figure 5-10.

Figure 5-10   Design Class with Operation

A.5.5

There is another way to quickly add elements to the design class diagram. If the mouse is positioned on top of the class, a menu of choices is displayed, such as Attribute (the little red square) and Operation (the green circle). Picking one of the choices will quickly add that element to the diagram (see Figure 5-11).

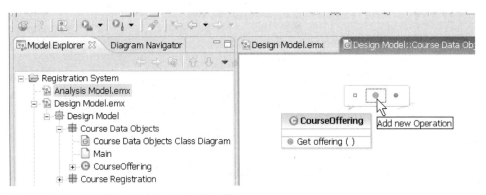

Figure 5-11   Quickly Add Design Class Elements

Information about the design elements can be entered as needed for design. As the design evolves, more information should be added to the class. At this stage of the design, no additional information has been added for the "Get offering information" operation method, as shown in Figure 5-12.

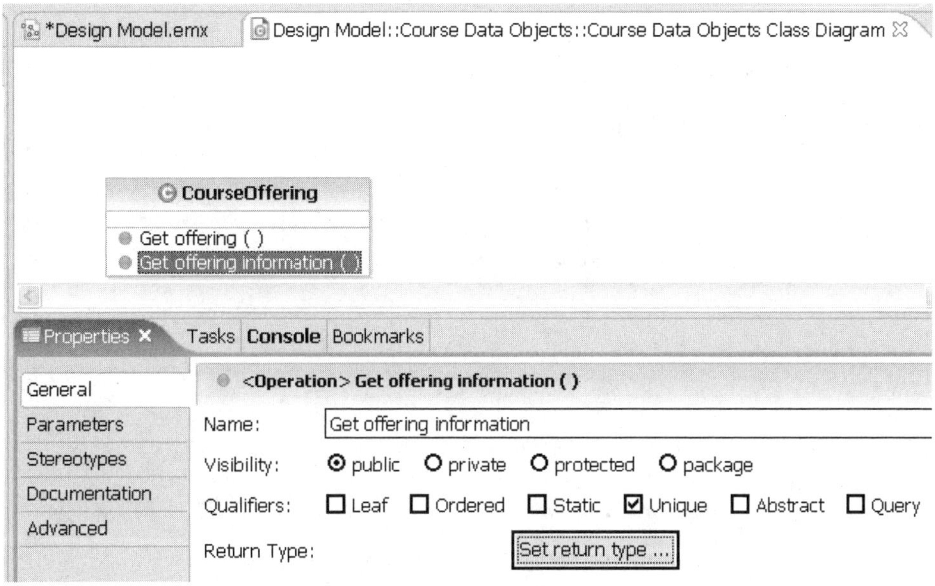

Figure 5-12   *Operation Information*

As mentioned, entity classes often transfer directly from the analysis model to the design model. Since the entity class is already defined with attributes and operations, it would be nice to simply copy the entity class from the analysis model to the design model.

COPYING FROM THE ANALYSIS MODEL

1. From the Model Explorer, right-click on the analysis entity class you wish to copy and select Copy.

2. In the Model Explorer, right-click on the design package to which you want to copy the class and select Paste.

This will copy the analysis class to the design package, as shown in Figure 5-13.

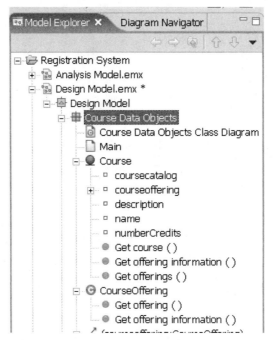

Figure 5-13   *Copied Analysis Class*

Note that this is still an analysis class. In order to change it to the desired design class, its sterotype must be changed. As stated before, the UML has a concept called a stereotype, which provides the capability of extending the basic modeling elements to create new elements.

CHANGING THE STEREOTYPE RELATIONSHIP

1. From the Model Explorer, select the class whose stereotype you wish to change.
2. In the Properties view, select the Stereotype tab.
3. Click the stereotype to be removed.
4. Click Remove Stereotypes.

This will remove the stereotype, as shown in Figure 5-14.

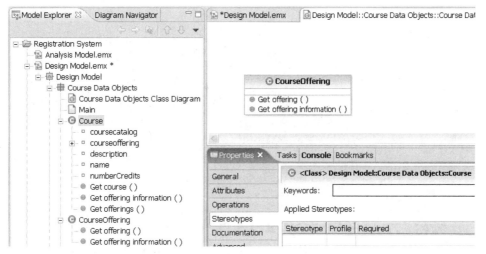

Figure 5-14   Design Class

However, something else came along when the analysis class was copied: the analysis model association relationship between Course and CourseOffering. This is shown in Figure 5-15.

We can visualize this relationship by simply adding it to our diagram.

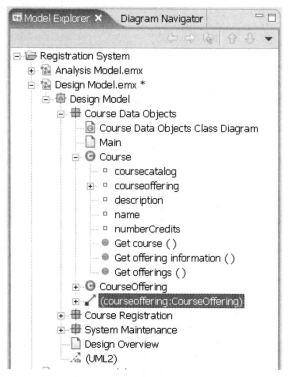

Figure 5-15   Analysis Relationship

VISUALIZING A RELATIONSHIP

1. From the Model Explorer, right-click the relationship you want to visualize and select Visualize > Add to Current Diagram.

This will add the relationship to the current diagram, as shown in Figure 5-16.

Note that this shows a relationship between the analysis class CourseOffering and the design class Course. This is not a valid relationship. Also, at analysis time, adding relationships to the Course class added some new attributes, as shown in the Properties view (see Figure 5-17).

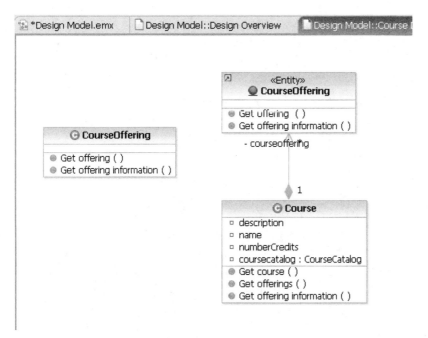

Figure 5-16   Visualized Relationship

	Default Value	Name	Is Static	Type	Visibility
□		description	false		private
□		name	false		private
□		numberCredits	false		private
□		coursecatalog	false	Class CourseCatalog	private
□		courseoffering	false	Class CourseOffering	private

Figure 5-17   Copied Attributes

We need to delete the elements we don't want (the
relationship to the analysis class) while keeping those things
we do want. At this point in time, you might be wondering
why we bothered copying this analysis class to the design

model if we have to modify it. This is a matter of choice. Some people may prefer deleting extra attributes and operations versus re-entering them. However, care must be taken when copying the attributes and operations to make sure they are examined in the context of the design model and to evaluate whether these attributes and operations should remain in the design model.

Rational Software Architect has the capability to transform from model to model (or model to code) so that, for example, UML classes in the source model with a stereotype of RUPAnalysis::Entity generate UML classes in the target classes with the appropriate changes (for example, changing the stereotype, copying all operations, attributes, and relationshops from source to target model, etc.). That is outside the scope of this book, but samples and tutorials are available at the IBM developerWorks site.

DELETING EXTRA ELEMENTS

1. In the Model Explorer, right-click the relationship to be deleted (courseoffering:CourseOffering) and select Delete from Model.

2. In the Design Model Class diagram, right-click the CourseOffering analysis class (identified by the < <Entity> > label) and select Delete from Diagram.

Seeing the association from the analysis models reminds us we need to also examine the analysis model relationships and determine how we want to model those in design. An analysis model relationship can become a design model relationship or even a design class. For example, if the only way to access the CourseOffering from Course was to go through a series of manipulations and accesses, we might represent the composition relationship as a class.

ADDING A RELATIONSHIP

1. In the class diagram, position the mouse pointer over the source class and wait for the arrow lines to be displayed (see Figure 5-18).

2. Click the outgoing arrow and drag it to the target class.

3. Select Create New Composition Association.

This will add the relationship, as shown in Figure 5-19.

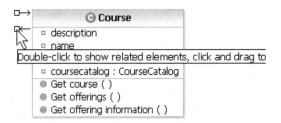

Figure 5-18   Quickly Creating a Relationship

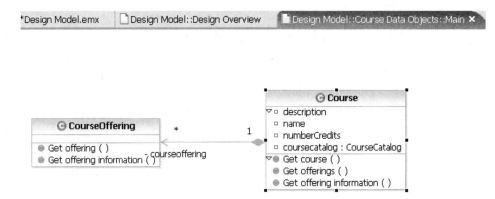

Figure 5-19   Relationship Added

Notice that when the design model relationship was created, a new attribute, courseoffering, was added to the Course class. This is shown in the Properties view in the Attributes section. This attribute is visualized as the relationship in the class diagram and in fact can be used during implementation as the unique identifier between Course and CourseOffering.

In the analysis model, we did not have to worry about the implementation details such as how we will achieve persistence and how relationships will be realized. This is one of the key differences between analysis and design. In design we must begin to take implementation details into account, although not to the level of writing code.

USER INTERFACES

USER INTERFACES ARE modeled at analysis time as boundary classes. A boundary class can be mapped to a page class at design time. If the boundary class involves inputting information, you would typically associate it with a form through aggregation. A form can be modeled as a nested class of the page, since its entire life cycle is governed by the client page. The way the Registration System is designed, the forms always have a submit relationship to a server page, which processes the form's values, ultimately leading to a new returned client page design.

At design time, try not to align yourself too closely with any one interface technology or implementation unless there are good reasons for doing so. For example, even through today we envision the forms being Web pages in a typical website, next year we might want to make it possible to select courses through a voice response system or using Web pages displayed on a mobile phone. By delaying the actual implentation decision as long as possible, we can build more flexibility into the design.

In practice, the design of the user interface is performed in combination with prototyping of the user interface. The user interface should be exposed to other people, especially end users, to make sure it meets their needs and expectations. Everyone wants an "easy to use" interface, but that often means different things to different types of users.

For that reason, the user interface design is usually not considered complete prior to prototyping that design. Often, you will defer detailed user interface design until after a few prototypes have been reviewed and honed. For the ESU Course Registration System we will at least do some initial design on the user interface.

Initial UI Design

A.5.6
A.5.7

For this example, we will look at just the Course Registration package in the analysis model and in fact just the Browse Course Catalog scenario. The boundary classes identified are as follows:

- BrowseCatalogHome
- CourseList
- CourseOfferingDetail
- CourseOfferingList

That's a good start—but we really need to know how these boundary classes are used. For that information, we need to examine the analysis model sequence diagrams.

The Browse Course Catalog sequence diagram shows us that the initial boundary class is the BrowseCatalogHome, and we can envision a screen of some sort where the user enters search criteria.

We also see that CourseOfferingDetail is accessed from CourseList. When one boudary class directly accesses another boundary class, perhaps they can be combined into one design class at design time, mapping to one form.

So, an initial first pass at design time would be to have one form to enter the search criteria and another to display the results and optionally display more detail on a given result.

Package Structure

With interfaces, we are getting close to implementation. If you are certain of the target implementation platform, you might consider using package names that are valid in the target implementation platform to avoid having to do namespace mapping. However, keep in mind that if a different target implemention is used, you will then have to do the namespace mapping anyway. A good initial pass would be a mapping back to the analysis model use cases structure, again realizing that this will evolve over time. Figure 5-20 shows the design model Course Registration package populated with the initial interface packages.

Now, just like we did for the entity classes, copy the boundary classes from the analysis model to the design model and remove the stereotype. Alternatively, you can create the classes and add the operations by hand.

In either case, to visualize this design once the classes are created, rename the Main diagram in the browse package to User Interface Diagram and drag and drop the boundary classes onto it (see Figure 5-21).

Next create the page class mapping to the boundary classes using the User Interface Diagram (see Figure 5-22).

Note that only two classes were created, as the CourseOffering and CourseOfferingDetail boundary classes will be represented as one page.

Finally, create the associations from the boundary classes to the page classes. This can be done quickly using the User Interface Diagram (see Figure 5.23).

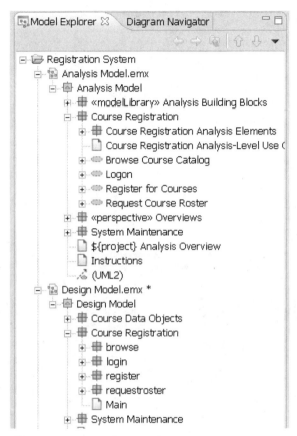

Figure 5-20   Interface Packages

Figure 5-21   User Interface Diagram

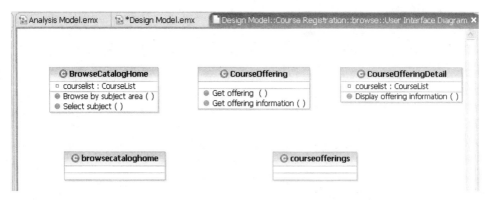

Figure 5-22   Added Page Classes

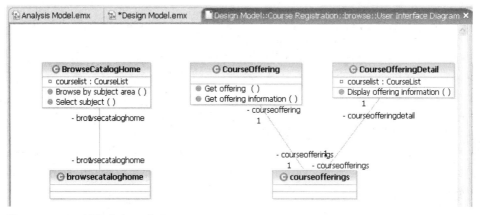

Figure 5-23   Added Associations

Depending on how many page classes and pages there are, you might want to create a navigation diagram with the various navigation paths laid out. The use case model activity diagram is a good place to start.

For the ESU Course Registration System Browse Course Catalog scenario, there are only a few page classes/pages, so the activity diagram from the use case model can be used to represent page flow. For this system, this is really as far as we need to go in terms of modeling the user interface because we will go through some prototypes during implementation.

SUMMARY

THE DESIGN MODEL is an object model describing the realization of the analysis model, and is used to conceive as well as document the design of the software system.

During design, analysis classes get transformed into various types of design elements.

Class diagrams are used during design to lay out the structure for implementation.

User interfaces are modeled as boundary classes at analysis time and get mapped into design classes for various parts of the user interface.

DEVELOPERWORKS LINKS

A.5.1 Crain, A. The simple artifacts of analysis and design. developerWorks, June 2004: http://www.ibm.com/developerworks/rational/library/4871.html

A.5.2 Franklin, S. Applying Rational tools to a simple J2EE-based project. Part 5: Architecture and design. developerWorks, December 2004: http://www.ibm.com/developerworks/rational/library/284.html

A.5.3 Marechaux, J-L. Developing a J2EE architecture with Rational Software Architect using the Rational Unified Process. developerWorks, August 2005: http://www.ibm.com/developerworks/rational/library/05/0816_Louis/

A.5.4 Bell, D. UML basics: The class diagram. developerWorks, September 2004. Chapter 1: http://www.ibm.com/developerworks/rational/library/content/RationalEdge/sep04/bell/

A.5.5 Tooke, M. Creating effective UML diagrams has never been easier. developerWorks, October 2005. Chapter 2: http://www.ibm.com/developerworks/rational/library/05/1011_tooke/

A5.6 Padilla, M. Strike a balance: Users' expertise on interface design. developerWorks, September 2003. Chapter 3: http://www.ibm.com/developerworks/web/library/wa-ui/

A5.7 Jones, W. Saving the task from the tool: Techniques for user experience requirements analysis. developerWorks, May 2002: http://www.ibm.com/developerworks/rational/library/2799.html

Implementation Model

THE IMPLEMENTATION MODEL represents the physical composition of the implementation in terms of Implementation subsystems and implementation elements (directories and files, including source code, data, and executable files). The implementation subsystem is a way to reduce complexity in an implementation model containing hundreds of elements. A good way to think of the implementation subsystem is as the implementation model version of the design package. Like all the model-to-model mappings, the implementation model can be mapped very closely or very loosely to the design model. However you decide, it is best to keep the mapping one to one; that is, one design package should be mapped to one implementation subsystem. This allows for easy and seamless traceability from design to code.

The Rational Software Architect theory of operation is to use platform-neutral models through design and then have Rational Software Architect transform these designs, through model-to-code transformations, into code or implementation levels. As needed, the design can be updated and the changes transformed again into code. Then, at the code level, Rational Software Architect allows you to simply visualize the code in a UML format.

PERSISTENCE CHOICES

IMPLEMENTATION IS WHERE the choices for persistence are realized. This is not to say that these decisions were not made earlier, but from a modeling point of view the design model should be persistence agnostic as much as possible in order to keep your options open. However, during implementation, persistence is no longer conceptual and must be realized through a variety of means. For many applications, persistence is achieved through storing information in a relational database. However, many times persistence of information is accomplished through the use of enterprise information systems such as CICS or IMS. The number of choices for persistence, and therefore the number of application programming interfaces (APIs), keeps growing.

For the ESU Course Registration System, the information is stored in a relational database. During development we will use IBM DB2 Universal Database (a copy for development purposes is supplied with Rational Software Architect), although since the database is relatively simple, almost any database would work.

A.6.1

Figure 6-1 shows the database layout for a portion of the ESU Course Registration System. Note that Rational Software Architect also includes some data modeling capabilities and those were used to create this diagram. The Data Definition Language (DDL) statements to both create and populate the database are available from the book's Web page (http://www.ibmpressbooks.com/title/0321238087).

Database Layout

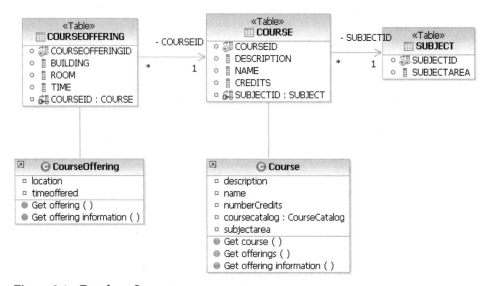

Figure 6-1   Database Layout

Once the persistence choice is made, another decision is how to access that persistence from the application. There is no shortage of options and frameworks, ranging from simple so-called data beans that encapsulate the Java Database Connectivity (JDBC) connections and calls to more sophisicated frameworks such as the J2EE standard Enterprise Java Bean (EJB) Entity Beans. Each has pluses and minuses, and the developer should weigh this decision carefully, taking into account the needs of the application, any enterprise standards, how long the application is expected to "live," the skill and experience of the development team, and so on. A good overview of object/relational persistence is provided in *Patterns of Enterprise Application Architecture*, by Martin Fowler (Boston: Addison-Wesley, 2003).

We will be examing the implementation for the Browse Course Catalog use case. As you may recall from the interface diagram in the design model, there are two pages: browsecataloghome and courseofferings. The main implementation details we will be concerned with are how to surface the database information onto the Web pages. We would prefer to shield the Web page developer from the details of how the data is retrieved.

SERVICE DATA OBJECTS

SERVICE DATA OBJECTS (SDO) is an open standard specification for a programming model that not only provides uniformity among data sources, but also does the following:

- Provides robust support for common application patterns

- Enables applications, tools, and frameworks to more readily query, bind, view, update, and introspect data

The goal is to simplify access to various data types and expose a common API to developers and tools. There are three main components involved:

- The data source

- The SDO datagraph

- The data source mediator

The *data source* is the place where data is stored. It can be just about anything—relational databases accessed through JDBC, EJBs, enterprise information systems such as CICS or IMS, or XML documents.

The *SDO datagraph* is a disconnected, source-independent, and structured result set. The datagraph is independent of connections to the originating data store. The datagraph also can identify and remember changes made from its original state. This capability allows the mediator to easily extract changes and move them to a data source. The datagraph structure is independent of data sources. In fact, different data source types can produce identical datagraphs. This feature unifies the client-programming model and allows for the creation of GUI tools that can work identically across different data source types.

The *data source mediators* are components that provide access to a specific data source type. They create SDO datagraphs by reading data from the data source, then propagating updates to the datagraphs back to the data source. Clients of the SDO runtime use a mediator specific to the data source type to retrieve a datagraph. Clients can then work with the data contained in the graph and make changes.

Mediators need to be configured to provide the desired functionality. This configuration information is referred to as the mediator's *metadata*. The metadata contains a variety of information, such as:

- The source-specific data artifacts being accessed
- A selection of fields that the applications will typically use
- The filters that apply selection criteria on retrievable data
- The actions to perform on the data source

Sometimes a picture is worth a thousand words. See Figure 6-2 for a high-level diagram of Service Data Objects.

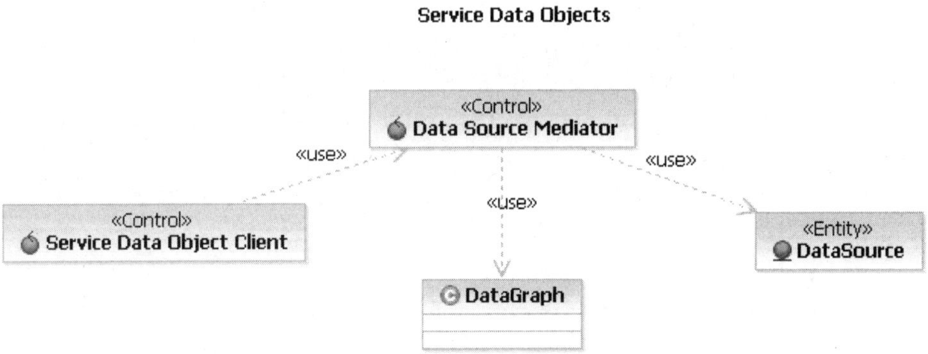

Service Data Objects

Figure 6-2   Service Data Object Diagram

In short, SDO simplifies development, providing one unique API to access heterogeneous data sources. From a development point of view, this means we only have to learn one API to access these disparate data sources. This is also good from a tool point of view because a development tool only has to work with one API to access these data sources.

USER INTERFACE CHOICES

A.6.2

THERE ARE MANY choices when it comes to the user interface. Two that come to mind immediately are a self-contained rich client user interface and a Web-based user interface. The rich client user interface typically offers a richer, more powerful set of controls with a large amount of local processing on the user's computer. The Web-based user interface typically provides very simple controls, such as text boxes, drop-down boxes, and buttons, with the bulk of the processing occurring on the server.

Each has pluses and minuses. A rich client user interface will usually offer more functionality and can take better advantage of the native capabilities of the platform. However, a rich client implies the installation and maintenance of that program on the client device as well as different versions of the program for different devices, and this is not always desired or practical. A Web-based user interface will typically offer less functionality and tends to be less sophisticated. Note that more recent programming models have started to change this so Web-based user interfaces are becoming more capable. Also, Web browsers are fairly universal, and installation and maintenance is required only at the server versus for each client. A well-layered system will separate the user interface from the rest of the system so that the choice of the user interface layer has no impact on the rest of the system, and thus the user interface can evolve as required. In fact, a properly layered system can support multiple user interface choices with minimal impact on the other layers.

A.6.3

For the ESU Course Registration System, we want users to be able to access the system from any system at any time, requiring only a connection to the Internet. This means a Web-based user interface. The next decision we need to make is which Web application framework to use. There are a number of popular ones, including Java Web frameworks such as Apache Struts and JavaServer Faces, .NET's ASP.NET, and Ruby on Rails. A Web application framework is a set of tools that make it easier to develop Web applications. The application is easier to debug, easier to extend, and easier to understand.

Struts is a popular framework from the Apache Software Foundation. The centerpiece of Struts is its model-view-controller (MVC)-style controller, which integrates with other technologies that provide the model and the view.[1] For the model, Struts can interact with standard data access technologies such as JDBC and EJB. For the view, Struts works well with JSP, including the JSP Standard Tag Library (JSTL) and JavaServer Faces (JSF) and other presentation systems.

A.6.4

Rational Software Architect has good support for building Struts-based Web applications. However, Struts is slowly falling out of favor for new applications, a victim of its own success. It became so popular that its shortcomings were magnified. For example, Struts does not come with a very rich set of user interface components. One of the strengths of Struts is its sophisticated page flow framework. The ESU Course Registration System will not be very complex, so we really don't need this level of sophistication. Finally, looking to the future, we might want the flexibility to render something besides standard HTML if we want to support other devices or markup languages, and Struts does not make provisions for that.

Obviously, the current and future needs of the application or enterprise will dictate what framework is used.

---

1. The model-view-controller design pattern, also known as Model 2 in J2EE application programming, is a well-established design pattern for programming. The model maintains the data, the view displays all or a portion of the data, and the controller handles events that affect the model or view.

Some enterprises even customize one of the frameworks for their own use with unique taglibs and components. The gains in productivity for doing this must be weighed against the cost of developing and maintaining these customizations.

JAVASERVER FACES

JAVASERVER FACES (JSF) is an open standard technology that helps you build user interfaces for dynamic Web applications that run on the server. The JSF framework manages user interface states across server requests and offers a simple model for the development of server-side events that are activated by the client. JSF is consistent.

The main components of JSF technology include:

- An extensive set of reusable user interface components

- A set of APIs for representing and managing user interface components, for handling events and input validation, and for defining page navigation

- A JavaServer Pages (JSP) custom tag library for expressing a JSF interface within a page

JSF is used to build Web applications. JavaServer Faces is also based on an MVC framework. For JSF, this means that the controller is a servlet, the model is represented by simple JavaBeans, and the view comprises JSF components with little or no application code. The goal of this model is to separate content from presentation.

Like many frameworks, the devil is in the details. You can certainly develop JSF-based applications "by hand," that is, hand coding all the files including the configuration files. However, many people will find that using a tool such as Rational Software Architect for JSF development is faster, quicker, and less error prone. Rational Software Architect supports dragging and dropping a set of standard JSF widgets that make building JSF-based pages easy.

The standard JSF renderer is for HTML. That is, there is a JSF life cycle that controls the processing of JSF requests. The last phase is to render the response into a form that can be used by the requesting client, and the standard renderer transforms the response into HTML. However, JSF is flexible enough so that other renderers could be written for other non-HTML clients as needed.

As with any technology, a best practice is to begin JSF development by hand and then move to using the tools once the programming model is understood. If you do not learn the programming model at the beginning, you will eventually hit situations where that knowledge is needed. It's a case of pay now or pay later. For this book, we will just use the tools and not cover the details. For readers interested in more detail on JSF, a great reference is chapter 18, "Using JavaServer Faces Technology in JSP Pages," from *The J2EE™ Tutorial, Second Edition*, by Stephanie Bodoff et al. (Boston: Addison-Wesley, 2004) or *Core JavaServer Faces*, by Geary and Horstmann (Sun Microsystems Press Java Series, 2004).

A.6.5

Given the nature of the ESU Course Registration System, JSF is an appropriate choice. We want to maintain flexibility for future device types, we want to take advantage of some of the rich user interface components of JSF, our Web page navigation will not be complex, and we want a simple development experience.

TYING IT TOGETHER

NOW THAT WE have covered the concepts, let's get to work. As noted, we have decided to use JSF and Service Data Objects. For the Browse Course Catalog use case, we also know we will need to create two pages (browsecataloghome and courseofferings). These pages need to exist inside a dynamic Web project, and, of course, a dynamic Web project will need to be part of a J2EE Enterprise project. Working on dynamic Web pages means we will have to enable the Web development capabilities of Rational Software Architect.

CREATING A WEB PROJECT

1. Click File > New > Other, and select Dynamic Web Project. Click the Next button. When asked, confirm the enablement of Web development capabilities.
2. Give the Web project a meaningful name, such as ESUCourseRegistration. Using blanks, spaces, or special characters is not recommended.
3. Click the Finish button.
4. When asked, switch to the Web perspective.

By expanding Enterprise Application and Dynamic Web Projects in the Project Explorer in the Web perspective as shown in Figure 6-3, we can see what was created. There is the enterprise application ESUCourseRegistrationEAR containing the dynamic Web project ESUCourseRegistration, and of course, the dynamic Web project itself.

Now that we have the basic structure, it's time to fill it out. There are a number of ways to do this within Rational Software Architect. One way that allows you to see the relationship of JSF pages to one another is the Web diagram. A Web application diagram, or Web diagram, is a file that helps you visualize and change the flow of a Web application such as a JSF or Struts-based application. The Web diagram editor is a visual editor for editing Web diagrams. Many frameworks rely on XML configuration files that are per-

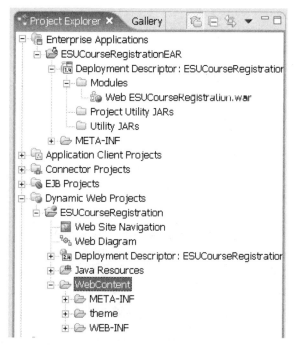

Figure 6-3   Initial Dynamic Web Project

fectly fine for computers to read but which are hard for people to read and edit. The Web diagram editor updates the XML configuration files, allowing you to work at a higher level of abstraction.

To open the Web diagram editor, in the Project Explorer, double-click on Dynamic Web Projects > ESUCourse-Registration > Web Diagram. This displays an "empty" Web diagram that displays some initial help, as shown in Figure 6-4.

A Web diagram consists of nodes and connections between nodes. A node is an icon that represents a resource such as a Web page, Java bean, or Web application.

If the resource exists, the node is called *realized*. If the resource does not exist, the node is called *unrealized*. That is, if the Web page is not yet created, it is unrealized. Realized

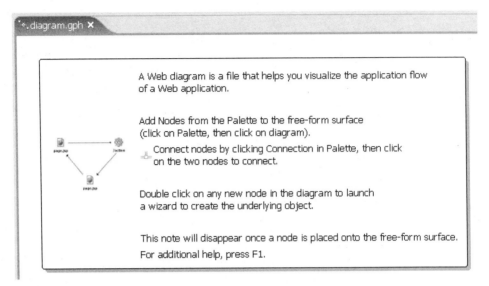

Figure 6-4   "Empty" Web Diagram

nodes are shown in color with their names in boldface. Unrealized nodes are shown as gray icons.

Remembering our design, we need to add two Web pages (two nodes) to the diagram.

ADDING WEB PAGES

1. From the palette area to the right of the Web diagram, right-click Web Page (in the Web Parts) folder.
2. Position the mouse pointer over the Web diagram (as shown in Figure 6-5).
3. Right-click to drop the new Web page onto the Web diagram.
4. Enter a file name such as browsecataloghome (note that you don't have to type .jsp; that is entered for you).

5. Repeat these steps for a second Web page called courseofferings so the Web diagram looks like Figure 6-6.

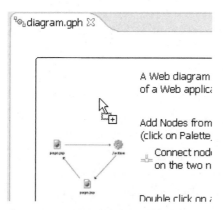

Figure 6-5   Dropping a Web Page

Figure 6-6   Web Diagram with Pages

Remember that nothing has been created because all the resources are unrealized and thus are displayed as gray icons or dotted lines. Let's create the Web pages.

CREATING WEB PAGES

1. In the Web diagram, double-click on browsecatalog-home.jsp.
2. Click on Finish.[2]
3. Delete the text "Place content here."
4. Return to the Web diagram and repeat these steps for courseofferings.jsp to create it.

If you look at the Web diagram, both browsecatalog-home.jsp and courseofferings.jsp are shown with color and boldfaced names, because they now exist.

Now, as you may recall from the design model Interface Diagram, users enter their search criteria on the browse-catalog screen, and the search criteria are by subject. We could have users type in a subject area and do a text search, but that would mean either the users would have to know the subject areas in advance and type them in correctly or our application would have to do some complicated text-matching algorithm. Neither is appealing for this applica-tion. It would be better if we presented users with a list of subjects and let them select the subject from the list. We could create the list from the subjects we know about today, but this would mean that when a new subject was added, we would have to change the list. This makes our applica-tion less flexible and more brittle. Instead, it would be nice if we could create a list of subjects on the fly as the applica-tion is running. From a database implementation point of view, this means we should have a table of subject areas and a relationship between the course table and the subject areas table. This has been done for the ESU database system.

---

2. Some levels of Rational Software Architect will require you to click on Configure Advanced Options prior to enabling the Finish button.

The ideal implementation would hide these details from the Web page so the Web page would not have to change regardless of how the database tables are structured. As discussed earlier, Service Data Objects can abstract out the details of the persistance model, so we will use Service Data Objects for interacting with the database. Advanced JSF developers could create custom JSF components that would allow page designers to drop in custom controls and further customize the controls via XML attributes (as opposed to having to write lots of generic tags or complex logic in JSP pages).

Note that the steps in this next exercise assume IBM DB2 Universal Database as the database and would need to be modified slightly depending on the database you use. It also assumes the database has been created and matches Figure 6-1. Finally, these steps keep the default names when provided, although realistically you would use more meaningful names.

Make sure you are back in the Web perspective before you start.

CREATING A DATA CONNECTION AND A DATA OBJECT

1. Select browsecataloghome.jsp for editing.
2. Left-click in the Page Data area to the bottom left of the Web page editor and select New > Relational Record List. This will start the Relational Record List wizard.
3. On the Relational Record List page of the Add Relational Record List wizard, enter "subjectlist" as the name of the record list and click Next.
4. On the Record List Properties page of the Add Relational Record List wizard, click the New button to create a new connection to the database.

5. On the Select a Database page of the New Connection wizard, click Create New DB Connection.

6. On the Establish a Connection to a Database page of the New Database Connection wizard, click Next.

7. On the Specify Connection Parameters page of the New Database Connection wizard, select the appropriate Alias name, such as COURSECAT, and enter the appropriate security information, such as userid and password.

8. Click Test Connection and validate you can connect to the database. If not, correct any errors until you can connect.

9. Click Finish.

10. Back on the Select a Database page of the New Connection wizard, click Finish to finish creating the connection.

11. On the Record List Properties page of the Add Relational Record List wizard, select the table we want to connect to, in this case, the SUBJECT table, and click Next.

12. Note that you can select which columns from the database will be part of the data object. We will keep them all, so click Finish.

The service data object is created, as shown in Figure 6-7. Now we need to display the information from the service data object on the page. We will create a data table and bind the service data object fields to the data table fields. A data table is a JSF component used to display application data. It consists of one or more columns, each with a header area and a data area, the data area repeating for each record. We could add a data table and then bind the columns to the service data object manually, but we will instead drag and

Figure 6-7   Service data object

drop the service data object to the page and let Rational
Software Architect do this for us.

CREATING A DATA TABLE FROM A SERVICE DATA OBJECT

1. Click and hold the subjectlist table in the subjectlist
   service data object (not the service data object itself).

2. Position the mouse pointer over browsecatalog-
   home.jsp and release the mouse button.[3] This starts
   the Insert Record List wizard.

3. On the Configure Data Controls page of the Insert
   Record List wizard, deselect SUBJECTID. SUBJECTID
   is only used internally and does not have to be displayed to the user.

4. Change the label from Subjectarea to Subject Area
   and click Finish.

The data table is created and linked to the service data
object, as shown in Figure 6-8.

---

3. This will be referred to as "drag and drop" for the remainder of this chapter.

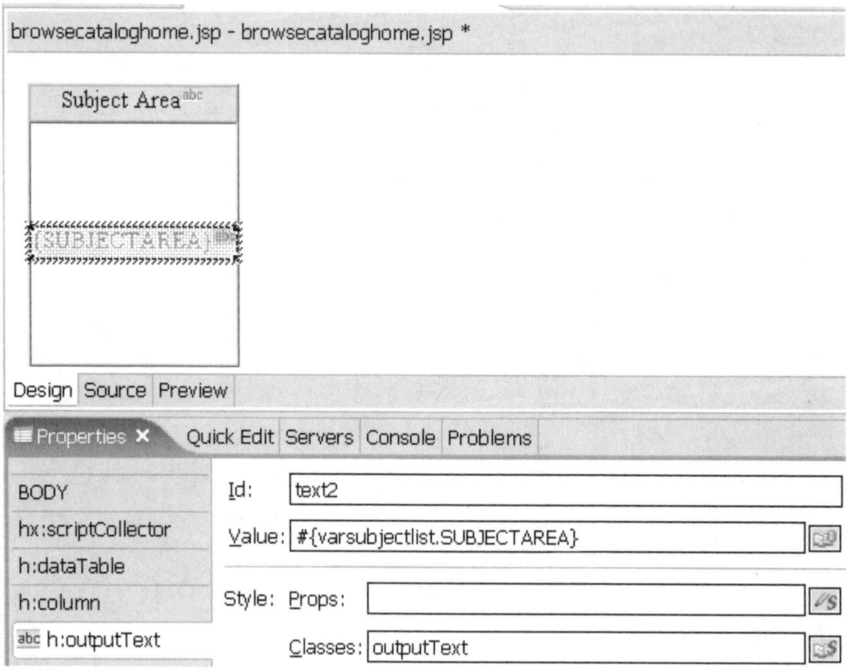

Figure 6-8   Data Table Bound to Service Data Object

Remembering the design, once a user selects a subject area, a page should be displayed with all the courses for that subject area, and once a user selects a course, that page should be refreshed with the course offerings for that course. While this can be done with JSF, we decide to make the interface a little less complicated for the first version in order to speed up development. Creating pages that refresh with an updated user interface takes more time to develop and test. These types of pragmatic decisions are made all the time, weighing various trade-offs. Each enterprise should have a process in place to govern whether or not these implementation decisions get back into the design.

Getting back to the actual implementation, we will first add a column to the data table and then add something called a command hyperlink to pass a parameter to the courseofferings.jsp page.

ADDING A COLUMN TO A DATA TABLE

1. In browsecataloghome.jsp, select the data table. This can be a little tricky, but try selecting anywhere in the data table and looking at the Properties view down at the bottom. If h:dataTable is not selected, select it in the Properties view (see Figure 6-9).

2. In the Columns area of the dataTable properties, click the Add button to add a new column.

3. Change the label for the column to Course Offerings (see Figure 6-10).

The data table has a new column.

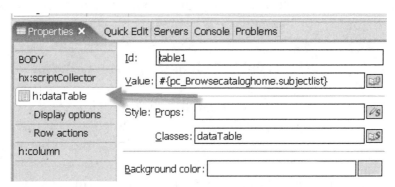

Figure 6-9   Selecting a Data Table

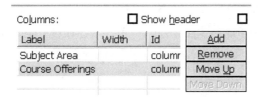

Figure 6-10   Adding a Column

ADDING A COMMAND HYPERLINK AND PARAMETER

1. In the Palette area of the page editor, click the Command – Hyperlink component in the Faces Components folder.
2. Position the mouse pointer in the column that was just added to the data table and click again.
3. Select the Command Link icon in the data table.
4. In the Properties view, under h:commandLink, click on Parameter and then click Add Parameter.
5. Change the name of the parameter from Name0 to ID.
6. Change the value of the parameter from Value0 by clicking Value0 and then clicking the Select Page Data Object icon that appears to the right of Value0.
7. On the Select Page Data Object page, expand subjectlist > subjectlist and select SUBJECTID (see Figure 6-11) and click OK.

This should result in the parameter being set as shown in Figure 6-12.

These steps created a clickable link for the data table and also specified a parameter to pass with the link, the parameter being the SUBJECTID of the subject the user clicks on.

The last thing we need to do for this page is to specify which page to display when the link is clicked.

SPECIFYING THE LINK PAGE

1. In the Properties view, click on h:commandLink.
2. In the Rules area of the Properties, click on Add Rule. . . .

Figure 6-11   Selecting a Parameter Variable

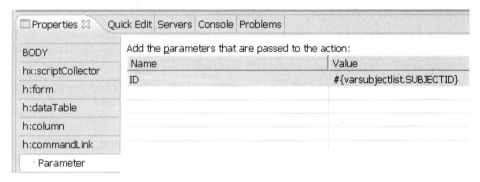

Figure 6-12   Parameter Setting

3. On the Add Navigation Rule page, use the drop-down arrow next to the Page input field to select courseofferings.jsp and click OK. Note that more complex rule conditions can be added.

4. In the Data Table, click "link label."

5. In the Properties view, change the Value from "link label" to "Display course offerings."

This should result in a browsecataloghome.jsp something like Figure 6-13.

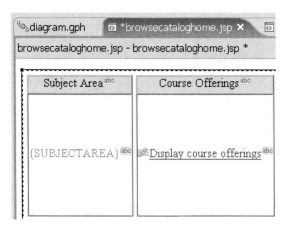

Figure 6-13   Completed browsecataloghome.jsp

Browsecataloghome.jsp is now complete, so we will turn our attention to courseofferings.jsp. The design tells us we should display all the course offerings for the selected subject area. We just added subject area ID as a parameter (called ID) to the command link for courseofferings.jsp, so we need to filter or limit the courses it displays to just those that have the same subject area ID.

CREATING A DATA OBJECT

1. Select courseofferings.jsp for editing.
2. Left-click in the Page Data area to the bottom left of the Web page editor and select New > Relational Record List. This will start the Relational Record List wizard.
3. On the Relational Record List page of the Add Relational Record List wizard, enter courselist as the name of the record list and click Next.

4. On the Record List Properties page of the Add Relational Record List wizard, ensure that the connection that was created for the earlier service data object is selected (the name should be something like ESUCourseRegistration Con1) and select the table we want to connect to (in this case, the COURSE table), and click Next.

5. On the Column Selection and Other Tasks page of the Add Relational Record List wizard, click the Filter Results link.

6. On the Filters page, click the big + symbol to add a new filter.

7. On the Conditions page, use the drop-down arrow to select the SUBJECTID column and enter #{param.ID} as the value (see Figure 6-14) and click OK.

8. Back on the Filters page, click Close.

9. Back on the Column Selection and Other Tasks page of the Add Relational Record List wizard, click Finish.

This creates a new service data object called courselist.

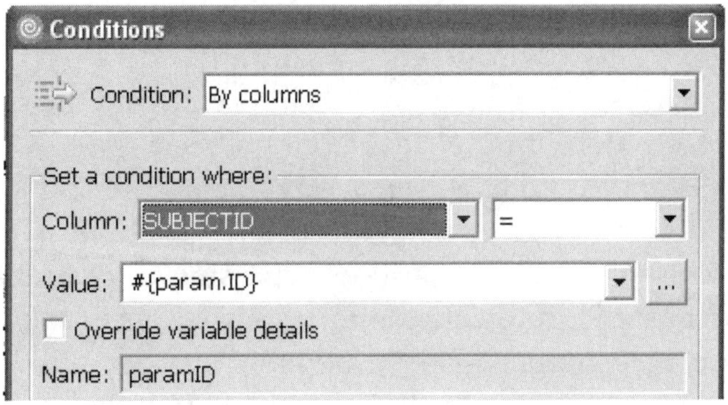

Figure 6-14   Entering a Filter

Drag and drop the new service data object onto courseofferings.jsp to create a new data table, displaying the columns as shown in Figure 6-15.

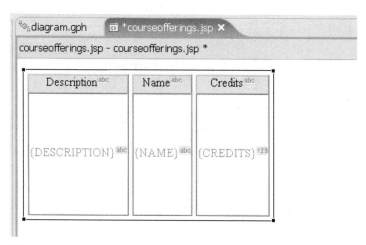

Figure 6-15   Courseofferings.jsp Data Table

Now is where we start deviating slightly from the design. When the user selects a course offering, we want to display a new page with the course offering details. Go back to editing the Web diagram (the file called diagram.gph). Add a new page called courseofferingsdetail.jsp and create it by double-clicking on it, again removing the default "place content here" text from the page.

We have to have some way to pass the course ID from courseofferings.jsp to courseofferingsdetail.jsp. Recall that we used automatic parameter passing between browsecatalaghome.jsp and courseofferings.jsp. This is only supported for the commandLink component, and we will be using a different component this time. One popular way to pass parameters is through the use of scripting variables. We will create a new scripting variable to pass the course ID from one page to the next.

CREATING A SCRIPTING VARIABLE

1. Select courseofferingsdetail.jsp for editing.

2. Left-click in the Page Data area to the bottom left of the Web page editor and select New > Scripting Variable > Session Scope Variable.

3. On the Add Session Scope Variable page, enter courseID for the variable name and java.lang.String for the variable type and click OK.

This will result in a new request scope variable, as shown in Figure 6-16.

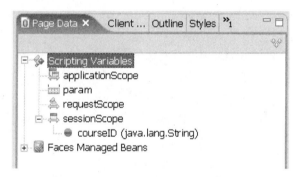

Figure 6-16   New Session Scope Variable

Next we will create a new service data object that will filter course offering details to just those courses.

CREATING A DATA OBJECT

1. Select courseofferingsdetail.jsp for editing.

2. Left-click in the Page Data area to the bottom left of the Web page editor and select New > Relational Record List. This will start the Relational Record List wizard.

3. On the Relational Record List page of the Add Relational Record List wizard, enter courseoffering as the name of the record list and click Next.

4. On the Record List Properties page of the Add Relational Record List wizard, ensure that the connection that was created for the earlier service data object is selected (the name should be something like ESUCourseRegistration_Con1) and select the table we want to connect to (in this case, the COURSE-OFFERING), table and click Next.

5. On the Column Selection and Other Tasks page of the Add Relational Record List wizard, click the Filter Results link.

6. On the Filters page, click the big + symbol to add a new filter.

7. On the Conditions page, use the drop-down arrow to select the COURSEID column and click the box with the three periods next to Value.

8. On the Select Page Data Object page, expand session-Scope and select courseID (see Figure 6-17) and click OK.

9. Back on the Conditions page, click OK.

10. Back on the Filters page, click Close.

11. Back on the Column Selection and Other Tasks page of the Add Relational Record List wizard, click Finish.

This creates a new service data object called courseoffering.

Drag and drop the new service data object onto courseofferingsdetail.jsp to create a new data table, displaying the columns as shown in Figure 6-18.

Save your work by pressing the Crtl, Shift, and S keys all at once. This saves all the changes on all files.

All that is left to do is to pass the parameter from courseofferings.jsp into the scripting variable. For this we

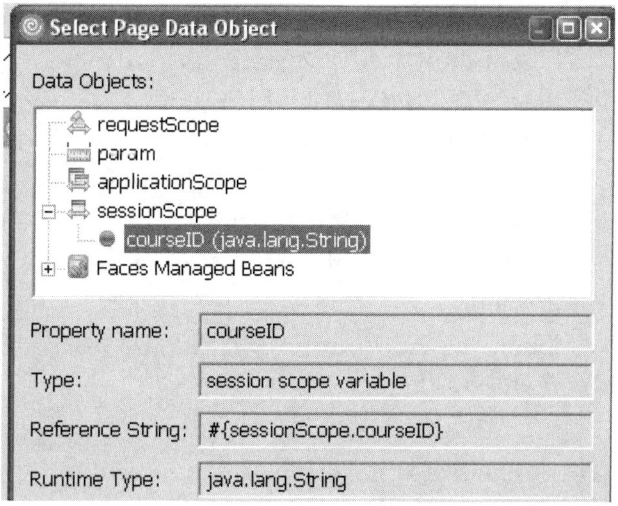

Figure 6-17   Selecting a Data Object

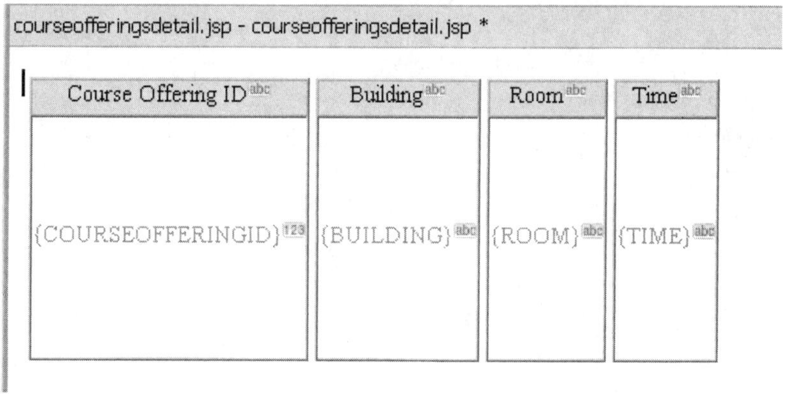

Figure 6-18   Courseofferingsdetail.jsp Data Table

will add a row action to the data table. This will allow the user to click anywhere on that row to perform an action— in this case, setting the scripting variable and displaying a new page with the course offering details on it.

First we will add a row action.

ADDING A ROW ACTION

1. Select courseofferings.jsp for editing.

2. Select the data table. This can be a little tricky, but try selecting anywhere in the data table and looking at the Properties view down at the bottom. If h:dataTable is not selected, select it in the Properties view.

3. Under h:dataTable in the Properties view, click Row actions.

4. Click the Add button for "Add an action that's performed when a row is clicked."

This creates a row action as shown in Figure 6-19. Press Ctrl + S to save this file.

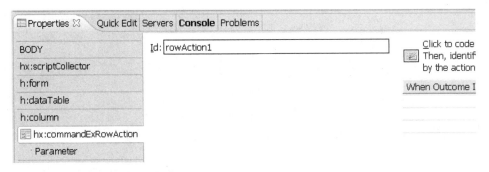

Figure 6-19   A New Row Action

Now, click on the QuickEdit button to switch to the QuickEdit view (see Figure 6-20).

Figure 6-20   Switching to QuickEdit

You will see a number of commented lines of Java code. These lines guide you through the process of adding the appropriate lines of Java code to pass parameters. We will add three lines of Java code to the bottom, just before the return instruction. Scroll to the bottom of the QuickEdit code and just before the `return ""`; line, add these three lines:

```
int row = getRowAction1().getRowIndex();
Object keyvalue =
    ((DataObject)getCourselist().get(row)).get("COURSEID");
getSessionScope().put("courseID",keyvalue);
```

The first line sets the variable row to the row number the user clicked on. The second line sets keyvalue to the COURSEID from that row (even though COURSEID is not displayed, it is present in the service data object). The third line puts that course ID into the script variable.

Finally, we will return a value for the JSF navigation map. Change the `return ""`; line to `return "displaydetails"`;.

The completed code should match Figure 6-21.

```
//     Specify the return value (a string) which is used by the navigation map to determine
//     the next page to display
int row = getRowAction1().getRowIndex();
Object keyvalue = ((DataObject)getCourselist().get(row)).get("COURSEID");
getSessionScope().put("courseID",keyvalue);
return "displaydetails";
```

Figure 6-21   Completed Code

We need to add a navigation rule for this page. Now, click on the Properties tab to move from the QuickEdit view to the Properties view. If commandExRowAction is not selected, select it.

ADDING A NAVIGATION RULE

1. Click on the Add Rule button to add a navigation rule.
2. On the Add Navigation Rule page, use the drop-down arrow to select courseofferingsdetail.jsp as the page.
3. Select the radio button next to "The outcome named" and enter displaydetails (see Figure 6-22) and click OK.

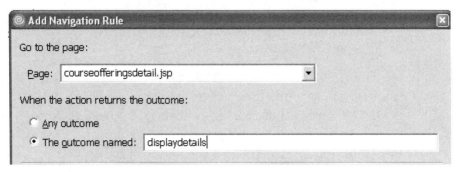

Figure 6-22   Adding a Navigation Rule

This creates a navigation rule, as shown in Figure 6-23.

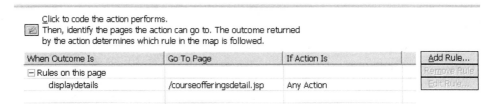

Figure 6-23   A Navigation Rule

Save your work by pressing the Ctrl, Shift, and S keys together.

Now to test our work. The following steps assume that the default WebSphere Application Server V6 was installed with Rational Software Architect.

TESTING THE APPLICATION

1. Go back to the Web diagram (diagram.gph).

2. Right-click on browsecataloghome.jsp and select Run on Server....

3. On the Define a New Server page, click Finish.

4. Once the server starts and browsecataloghome.jsp is displayed in the built-in browser, click on one of the "Display course offerings" links (see Figure 6-24).

5. This will display the courseofferings.jsp page in the built-in browser. Click on one of the rows (see Figure 6-25).

6. This will display the courseofferingsdetails.jsp page in the built-in browser (see Figure 6-26).

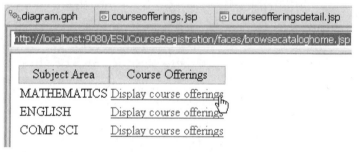

Figure 6-24   Running browsecataloghome

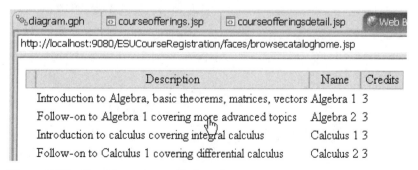

Figure 6-25   Running courseofferings.jsp

diagram.gph   courseofferings.jsp   courseofferingsdetail.jsp

http://localhost:9080/ESUCourseRegistration/faces/courseofferings.jsp

Course Offering ID	Building	Room	Time
10,100	Swain	301	T-T 09:30-10:45
10,101	Carroll	100	M-W-F 09:00-09:50
10,102	Sitterson	103	T-T 01:00-02:15

Figure 6-26   Running courseofferingsdetails.jsp

Well, the formatting of the Course Offering ID could be better, but that can be corrected by modifying the properties of the field.

We could easily imagine using another row action or command link for the actual course registration.

Finally, let's go back to the Web diagram. Right-click on browsecataloghome.jsp and select Draw > Draw All. This will show the various actions and links we added so the flow of the pages is better understood, as shown in Figure 6-27.

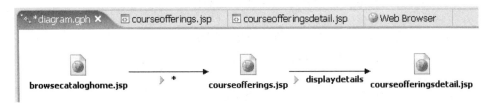

Figure 6-27   Updated Web Diagram

This completes this part of the implementation. This should be tested with potential end users to see if it meets their needs.

SUMMARY

THE IMPLEMENTATION MODEL represents the physical composition of the implementation in terms of implementation subsystems and implementation elements

The choice of persistence is an important decision that will most likely be influenced by existing standards, but the implementation should be layered in such as way that the persistence choice can be changed as needed. Service Data Objects is one such way.

There are a number of popular Web application frameworks with which you can build a Web application, including Struts and JavaServer Faces.

Rational Software Architect includes a number of capabilities that make creating data-centric Web applications fairly fast.

DEVELOPERWORKS LINKS

A.6.1   DB2 Universal Database support and trial software. developerWorks: http://www.ibm.com/developerworks/ downloads/im/udb/index.html?S_TACT = 105AGX28&S_CMP = DLMAIN

A.6.2   Service Data Object specification. developerWorks, November 2005: http://www.ibm.com/developerworks/ webservices/library/specification/ws-sdo/

A.6.3   Berry, D. The user experience, Part 1. developerWorks, February 2005: http://www.ibm.com/developer-works/web/library/w-berry2.html

A.6.4   Davis, M. Struts, an open source MVC implementation. developerWorks, February 2001: http://www.ibm.com/ developerworks/java/library/j-struts/

A.6.5   Hightower, R. JSF for nonbelievers (four-part series). developerWorks, starting February 2004: http://www.ibm.com/developerworks/java/library/j-jsf1/

Appendix

UML Metamodel

- UML Definition Documents

- Specification Document Structure

- Metamodel Structure

UML DEFINITION DOCUMENTS

THE UML IS defined by a set of documents published by the Object Management Group [UML-04]. These documents may be found on the OMG website (www.omg.org). They may be updated from time to time by the OMG. This appendix explains the structure of the UML semantic model described in the documents.

The UML is formally defined using a metamodel—that is, a model of the constructs in UML. The metamodel itself is expressed in UML. This is an example of a metacircular interpreter—that is, a language defined in terms of itself. Things are not completely circular. Only a small subset of UML is used to define the metamodel. In principle, this fixed point of the definition could be bootstrapped from a more basic definition. In practice, going to such lengths is unnecessary.

Each section of the semantic document contains a class diagram showing a portion of the metamodel; a text description of the metamodel classes defined in that section, with their attributes and relationships; a list of constraints on elements expressed in natural language and in OCL; and a text description of the dynamic semantics of the UML constructs defined in the section. The dynamic semantics are therefore informal, but a fully formal description would be both impractical and unreadable by most.

Notation is described in a separate appendix that references the semantics chapter on the OMG website and maps symbols to metamodel classes.

SPECIFICATION DOCUMENT STRUCTURE

THE UML IS defined in two complementary specifications, the UML 2.0 Infrastructure and the UML 2.0 Superstructure.

The infrastructure is intended to define foundational concepts that can be used in part or entirely by other specifications, for example, by the Meta-Object Specification (MOF) and Common Warehouse Metadata (CWM). It contains only the basic static concepts from UML and is oriented toward data structure description.

The UML superstructure defines the complete UML as experienced by users. There is a subset of the superstructure, called the kernel, that incorporates in the superstructure document all the relevant parts of the infrastructure. The superstructure specification is therefore self-contained, and readers usually will not have to read the infrastructure specification unless they are concerned about configuring other specifications in parallel to UML.

The rest of this appendix describes the organization of the UML superstructure specification.

METAMODEL STRUCTURE

THE METAMODEL IS divided into two main packages, structure and behavior, with two supporting packages, auxiliary elements and profiles (Figure A-1).

- The structure package defines the static structure of the UML. Within the structural package, the classes package is the foundation for everything else in UML.

- The behavior package defines the dynamic structure of the UML. Within this package, the common behavior package is not directly usable in models, but it defines the constructs shared by the other behavior subpackages.

- The auxiliary elements package defines concepts such as data types.

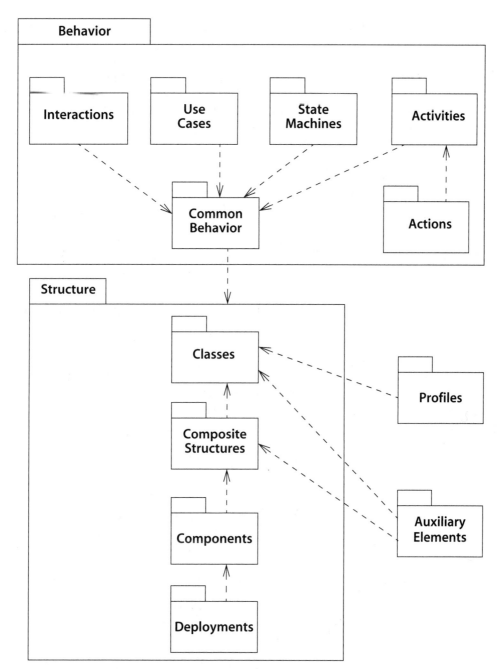

Figure A-1   Package Structure of the UML Metamodel

- The profiles package provides the ability to tailor UML

Each package is described by a chapter in the superstructure specification document. The views that we described in the overview to this book correspond roughly to the specification chapters.

Appendix B

Notation Summary

THIS APPENDIX CONTAINS a brief visual summary of notation. The major notational elements are included, but not every variation or option is shown. For full details, see the dictionary entry for each element.

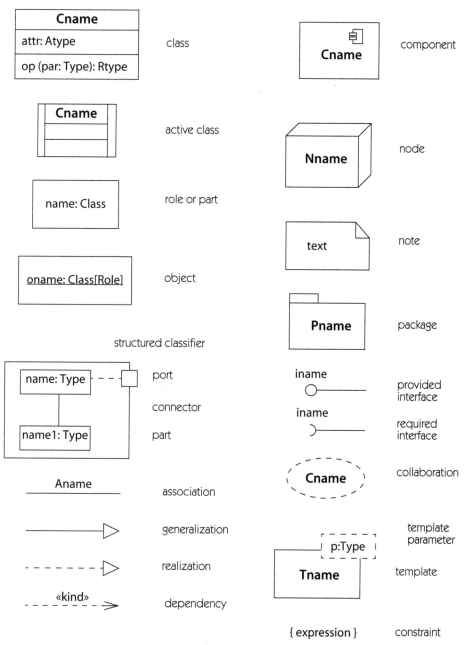

Figure B-1   Icons on Class, Component, Deployment, and Collaboration Diagrams

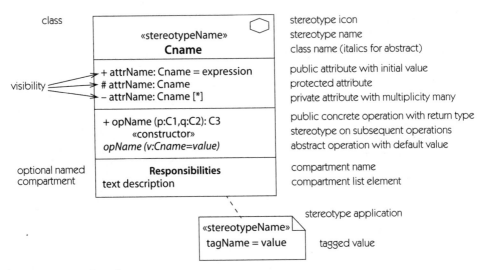

Figure B-2   Class Contents

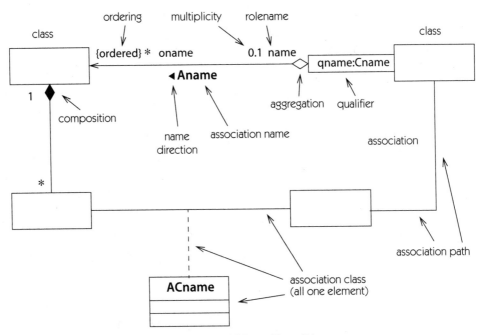

Figure B-3   Association Adornments Within a Class Diagram

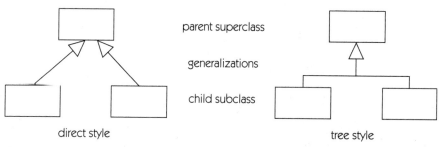

Figure B-4   Generalization

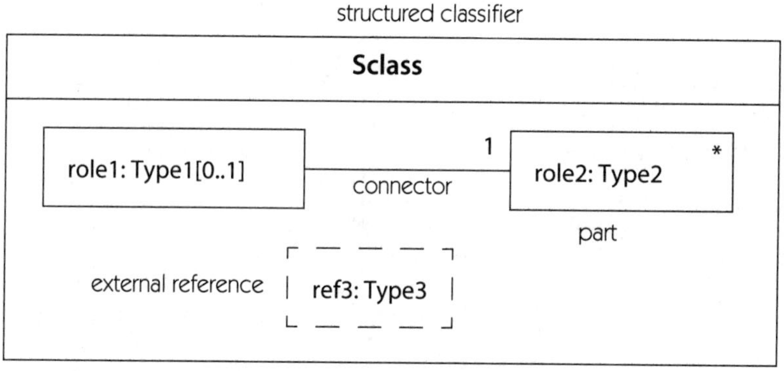

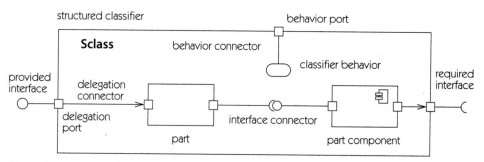

Figure B-5   Internal Structure: Parts and Connectors

Figure B-6   Internal Structure: Interfaces, Ports, and Internal Wiring

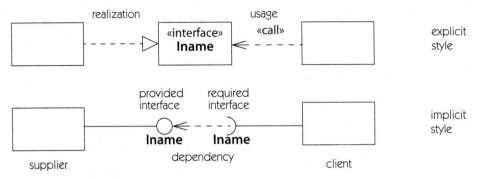

Figure B-7   Realization of an Interface

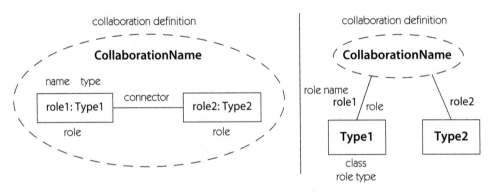

Figure B-8   Collaboration Definition—Alternate Notations

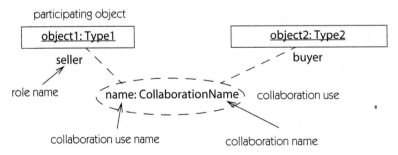

Figure B-9   Collaboration Use

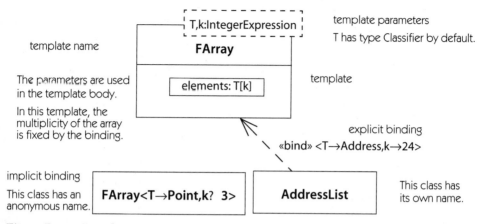

template name

template parameters
T has type Classifier by default.

The parameters are used in the template body.

In this template, the multiplicity of the array is fixed by the binding.

template

explicit binding
«bind» <T→Address,k→24>

implicit binding

This class has an anonymous name.

FArray<T→Point,k? 3>

AddressList

This class has its own name.

Figure B-10   Template

The package Y adds public contents of package Z to Y's namespace privately.

Y

+C

U

+A

«access»

Z

+D

−B   +C

package with nested subpackage and class

The package Z adds public contents of package X to Z's namespace. ⟶ | «import»

X

+E

−G   +F

The class G is private and accessible only inside package X. ⟶

Figure B-11   Package Notation

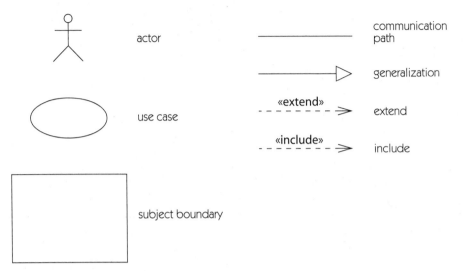

Figure B-12   Icons on Use Case Diagrams

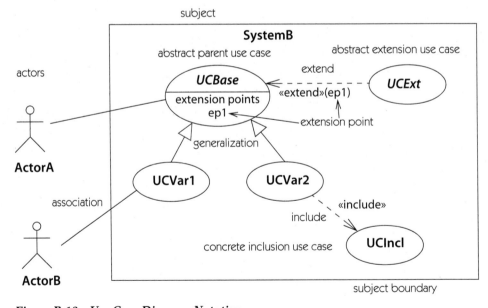

Figure B-13   Use Case Diagram Notation

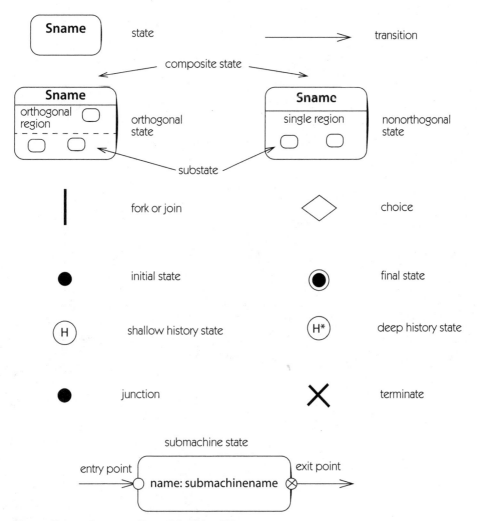

Figure B-14   Icons on State Machine Diagrams

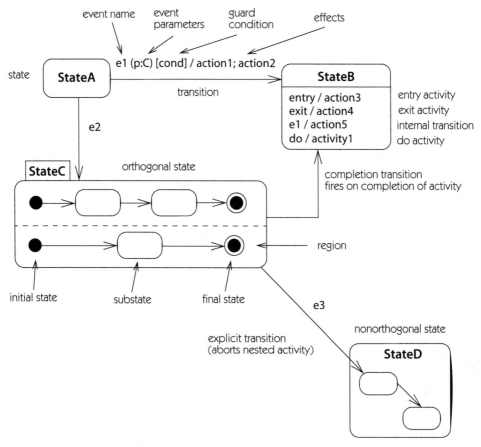

Figure B-15   State Machine Notation

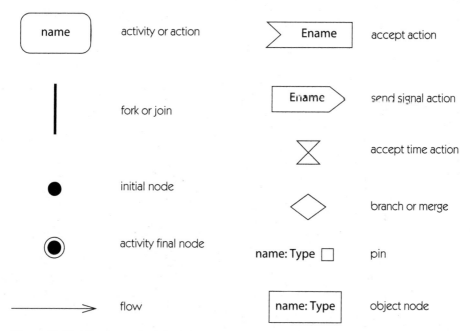

Figure B-16   Icons on Activity Diagrams

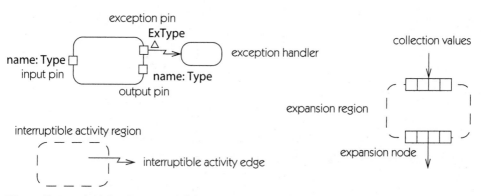

Figure B-17   Activity Groups and Icons

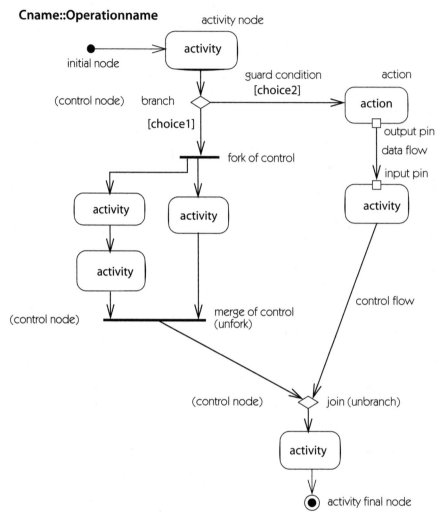

Figure B-18   Activity Diagram Notation

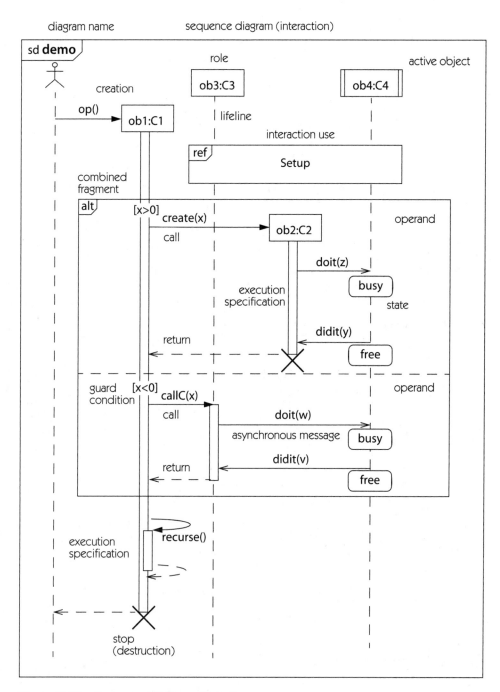

Figure B-19   Sequence Diagram Notation

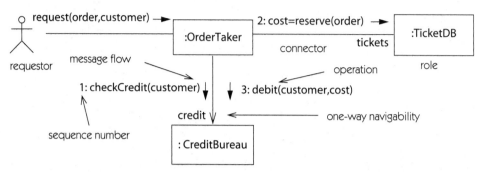

Figure B-20   Communication diagram notation

asynchronous message

synchronous call

return message

Figure B-21   Message Notation

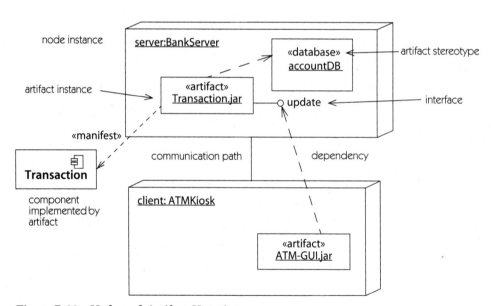

Figure B-22   Node and Artifact Notation

Index

Get
The
Rational
Edge

informIT

THIS BOOK IS SAFARI ENABLED

INCLUDES FREE 45-DAY ACCESS TO THE ONLINE EDITION

The Safari® Enabled icon on the cover of your favorite technology book means the book is available through Safari Bookshelf. When you buy this book, you get free access to the online edition for 45 days.

Safari Bookshelf is an electronic reference library that lets you easily search thousands of technical books, find code samples, download chapters, and access technical information whenever and wherever you need it.

TO GAIN 45-DAY SAFARI ENABLED ACCESS TO THIS BOOK:

- Go to **http://www.awprofessional.com/safarienabled**
- Complete the brief registration form
- Enter the coupon code found in the front of this book on the "Copyright" page

Addison
Wesley